# Great Teachers

# Great Teachers

## POPE BENEDICT XVI

Our Sunday Visitor Publishing Division
Our Sunday Visitor, Inc.
Huntington, Indiana 46750

Copyright © 2011 by Libreria Editrice Vaticana

Copyright © 2011 by Our Sunday Visitor Publishing Division,
Our Sunday Visitor, Inc. Published 2011.

16  15  14  13  12  11      1  2  3  4  5  6  7  8  9

ISBN 978-1-59276-536-2 (Inventory No. T1176)
LCCN: 2010942585

Interior design by M. Urgo
Cover design by Lindsey Riesen

Cover art: Detail of St. Dominic from *The Crucifixion*
by Angelico, Fra (Guido di Pietro) (c.1387-1455)
Museo di San Marco dell'Angelico, Florence, Italy / The Bridgeman Art Library
Nationality / copyright status: Italian / out of copyright

PRINTED IN THE UNITED STATES OF AMERICA

# TABLE OF CONTENTS

# CHAPTER ONE

# Monastic Theology and Scholastic Theology[1]

There is an interesting page of history that concerns the flourishing of Latin theology in the twelfth century that occurred through a series of providential coincidences. A relative peace prevailed in the countries of Western Europe at that time that guaranteed economic development and the consolidation of political structures in society, encouraging lively cultural activity also through its contacts with the East. The benefits of the vast action known as the "Gregorian reform" were already being felt within the Church. Vigorously promoted in the previous century, they had brought greater evangelical purity to the life of the ecclesial community, especially to the clergy, and had restored to the Church and to the Papacy authentic freedom of action. Furthermore, a wide-scale spiritual renewal supported by the vigorous development of consecrated life was spreading; new religious orders were coming into being and expanding, while those already in existence were experiencing a promising spiritual revival.

---

[1] Editor's note: The material in this book is derived from catecheses given by Pope Benedict XVI during his weekly general audiences from October 28, 2009, to July 7, 2010. The texts have been edited slightly to facilitate presentation in book form. The date each address was originally presented is annotated in the footnotes.

Theology also flourished anew, acquiring a greater aware-
ness of its own nature: it refined its method; it tackled the new
problems; advanced in the contemplation of God's mysteries;
produced fundamental works; inspired important initiatives of
culture, from art to literature; and prepared the masterpieces of
the century to come, the century of Thomas Aquinas and Bonaventure of Bagnoregio. This intense theological activity took
place in two milieus: the monasteries and the urban Schools,
the *scholae,* some of which were the forerunners of universities,
one of the characteristic "inventions" of the Christian Middle
Ages. It is on the basis of these two milieus, monasteries and
*scholae,* that it is possible to speak of the two different theological models: "monastic theology" and "scholastic theology." The
representatives of monastic theology were monks, usually abbots,
endowed with wisdom and evangelical zeal, dedicated essentially
to inspiring and nourishing God's loving design. The representatives of Scholastic theology were cultured men, passionate about
research; they were *magistri* anxious to show the reasonableness
and soundness of the Mysteries of God and of man, believed
with faith, of course, but also understood by reason. Their different finalities explain the differences in their method and in their
way of doing theology.

In twelfth-century monasteries the theological method
mainly entailed the explanation of Sacred Scripture, the *sacra
pagina* to borrow the words of the authors of that period; biblical
theology in particular was practiced. The monks, in other words,
were devout listeners to and readers of the Sacred Scriptures and
one of their chief occupations consisted in *lectio divina,* that is,
the prayed reading of the Bible. For them the mere reading of
the Sacred Text did not suffice to perceive its profound meaning,
its inner unity and transcendent message. It was therefore necessary to practice a biblical theology, in docility to the Holy Spirit.

Thus, at the school of the Fathers, the Bible was interpreted allegorically in order to discover on every page of both the Old and New Testaments what it says about Christ and his work of salvation.

The 2008 Synod of Bishops on the "Word of God in the life and mission of the Church" reminded us of the importance of the spiritual approach to the Sacred Scriptures. It is useful for this purpose to take into account monastic theology, an uninterrupted biblical exegesis, as well as the works written by its exponents, precious ascetic commentaries on the Books of the Bible. Thus monastic theology incorporated the spiritual aspect into literary formation. It was aware, in other words, that a purely theoretical and unversed interpretation is not enough: to enter into the heart of Sacred Scripture it must be read in the spirit in which it was written and created. Literary knowledge was necessary in order to understand the exact meaning of the words and to grasp the meaning of the text, refining the grammatical and philological sensibility. Thus *Jean Leclercq*, a Benedictine scholar in the past century, entitled the essay in which he presents the characteristics of monastic theology: *L'amour des lettres et le désir de Dieu* (Love of words and the desire for God). In fact, the desire to know and to love God, who comes to meet us through his words, to be received, meditated upon, and put into practice, leads us to seek to deepen our knowledge of the biblical texts in all their dimensions. Then there is another attitude on which those who practice monastic theology insist: namely an intimate, prayerful disposition that must precede, accompany, and complete the study of Sacred Scripture. Since, ultimately, monastic theology is listening to God's word, it is impossible not to purify the heart in order to receive it and, especially, it is impossible not to enkindle in it a longing to encounter the Lord. Theology thus becomes meditation, prayer, a song of praise, and impels us to sincere conversion. On this path, many exponents of monastic theology attained the highest goals of mystic experience and extend an invitation to us too to nourish our lives with the word of God, for example, through listening more attentively to the Readings and the Gospel, especially during Sunday Mass. It is also important to set aside a certain period each day for meditation on the Bible, so that the word of God may be a light that illumines our daily pilgrimage on earth.

Scholastic theology, on the other hand, as I was saying, was practiced at the *scholae* which came into being beside the great cathedrals of that time for the formation of the clergy, or around a teacher of theology and his disciples, to train professionals of culture in a period in which the appreciation of knowledge was constantly growing. Central to the method of the Scholastics was the *quaestio*, that is, the problem the reader faces in approaching the words of Scripture and of Tradition. In the face of the problem that these authoritative texts pose, questions arise and the debate between teacher and student comes into being. In this discussion, on the one hand the arguments of the authority appear and on the other those of reason, and the ensuing discussion seeks to come to a synthesis between authority and reason in order to reach a deeper understanding of the word of God. In this regard St. Bonaventure said that theology is *"per additionem"* (cf. *Commentaria in quatuor libros sententiarum*, I, *proem.*, q. 1, *concl.*), that is, theology adds the dimension of reason to the word of God and thus creates a faith that is deeper, more personal, hence also more concrete in the person's life. In this regard various solutions were found and conclusions reached which began to build a system of theology.

The organization of the *quaestiones* led to the compilation of ever more extensive syntheses, that is, the different *quaestiones* were composed with the answers elicited, thereby creating a synthesis, the *summae* that were in reality extensive theological and dogmatic treatises born from the confrontation of human reason with the word of God. Scholastic theology aimed to present the unity and harmony of the Christian Revelation with a method, called, precisely "Scholastic" of the school which places trust in human reason. Grammar and philology are at the service of theological knowledge, but logic even more so, namely the discipline that studies the "functioning" of human reasoning, in such a way that the truth of a proposal appears obvious. Still today, in reading the Scholastic *summae* one is struck by the order, clarity, and logical continuity of the arguments and by the depth of certain insights. With technical language a precise meaning is attributed to every word and, between believing and understanding, a reciprocal movement of clarification is established.

Dear brothers and sisters, in echoing the invitation of the First Letter of Peter, Scholastic theology stimulates us to be ever ready to account for the hope that is in us (cf. 3: 15), hearing the questions as our own and thus also being capable of giving an answer. It reminds us that a natural friendship exists between faith and reason, founded in the order of Creation itself. In the *incipit* of the Encyclical *Fides et Ratio*, the Servant of God John Paul II wrote: "Faith and reason are like two wings on which the human spirit rises to the contemplation of truth." Faith is open to the effort of understanding by reason; reason, in turn, recognizes that faith does not mortify her but on the contrary impels her toward vaster and loftier horizons. The eternal lesson of monastic theology fits in here. Faith and reason, in reciprocal dialogue, are vibrant with joy when they are both inspired by the search for intimate union with God. When love enlivens the prayerful dimension of theology, knowledge, acquired by reason, is broadened. Truth is sought with humility, received with wonder and gratitude: in a word, knowledge only grows if one loves truth. Love becomes intelligence and authentic theology wisdom of the heart, which directs and sustains the faith and life of believers. Let us therefore pray that the journey of knowledge and of the deepening of God's Mysteries may always be illumined by divine love.

# CHAPTER TWO

# Two Theological Models in Comparison: Bernard and Abelard[1]

In the last chapter I presented the main features of twelfth-century monastic theology and scholastic theology which, in a certain sense, we might call respectively "theology of the heart" and "theology of reason." Among the exponents of both these theological currents a broad and at times heated discussion developed, symbolically represented by the controversy between St. Bernard of Clairvaux and Abelard.

In order to understand this confrontation between the two great teachers it helps to remember that theology is the search for a rational understanding, as far as this is possible, of the mysteries of Christian Revelation, believed through faith: *fides quaerens intellectum* faith seeks understanding to borrow a traditional, concise, and effective definition. Now, whereas St. Bernard, a staunch representative of monastic theology, puts the accent on the first part of the definition, namely on *fides* faith, Abelard, who was a scholastic, insists on the second part, that is, on the *intellectus*, on understanding through reason. For Bernard faith itself is endowed with a deep certitude based on the testimony of Scripture and on the teaching of the Church Fathers. Faith, moreover, is reinforced by the witness of the saints and by the

---

[1] Pope Benedict XVI, General Audience, November 4, 2009.

inspiration of the Holy Spirit in the individual believer's soul. In cases of doubt and ambiguity, faith is protected and illumined by the exercise of the Magisterium of the Church.

So it was that Bernard had difficulty in reaching agreement with Abelard and, more in general, with those who submitted the truths of faith to the critical examination of the intellect; an examination which in his opinion entailed a serious danger, that is, intellectualism, the relativization of truth, the questioning of the actual truths of faith. In this approach Bernard saw audacity taken to the point of unscrupulousness, a product of the pride of human intelligence that claims to "grasp" the mystery of God. In a letter he writes with regret: "Human ingenuity takes possession of everything, leaving nothing to faith. It confronts what is above and beyond it, scrutinizes what is superior to it, bursts into the world of God, alters rather than illumines the mysteries of faith; it does not open what is closed and sealed but rather uproots it, and what it does not find viable in itself it considers as nothing and refuses to believe in it" (*Epistola* CLXXXVIII,1: *PL* 182, 1, 353).

Theology for Bernard had a single purpose: to encourage the intense and profound experience of God. Theology is therefore an aid to loving the Lord ever more and ever better, as the title of his Treatise on the Duty to love God says (*Liber de diligendo Deo*). On this journey there are various stages that Bernard describes in detail, which lead to the crowning experience when the believer's soul becomes inebriated in ineffable love. Already on earth the human soul can attain this mystical union with the divine Word, a union that the *Doctor Mellifluus* describes as "spiritual nuptials." The divine Word visits the soul, eliminates the last traces of resistance, illuminates, inflames, and transforms it. In this mystical union the soul enjoys great serenity and sweetness and sings a hymn of joy to its Bridegroom. As I mentioned in my catechesis on the life and doctrine of St. Bernard (in the book *The Fathers, Volume II*), theology for him could not but be nourished by contemplative prayer, in other words by the affective union of the heart and the mind with God.

On the other hand Abelard, who among other things was the very person who introduced the term "theology" in the sense in which we understand it today, puts himself in a different perspective. Born in Brittany, France, this famous teacher of the twelfth century was endowed with a keen intelligence and his vocation was to study. He first concerned himself with philosophy and then applied the results he achieved in this discipline to theology, which he taught in Paris, the most cultured city of the time, and later in the monasteries in which he lived. He was a brilliant orator: literally crowds of students attended his lectures. He had a religious spirit but a restless personality and his life was full of dramatic events: he contested his teachers, and he had a son by Héloïse, a cultured and intelligent woman. He often argued with his theological colleagues and also underwent ecclesiastical condemnations although he died in full communion with the Church, submitting to her authority with a spirit of faith. Actually St. Bernard contributed to condemning certain teachings of Abelard at the Provincial Synod of Sens in 1140 and went so far as to request Pope Innocent II's intervention. The Abbot of Clairvaux contested, as we have seen, the excessively intellectualistic method of Abelard who in his eyes reduced faith to mere opinion, detached from the revealed truth. Bernard's fears were not unfounded and were, moreover, shared by other great thinkers of his time. Indeed, an excessive use of philosophy dangerously weakened Abelard's Trinitarian teaching, hence also his idea of God.

In the moral field his teaching was not devoid of ambiguity: he insisted on considering the intention of the subject as the sole source for defining the goodness or evil of moral acts, thereby neglecting the objective significance and moral value of the actions: a dangerous subjectivism. This as we know is a very timely aspect for our epoch in which all too often culture seems to be marked by a growing tendency to ethical relativism; the self alone decides what is good for it, for oneself, at this moment. However, the great merits of Abelard, who had many disciples and made a crucial contribution to the development of scholastic theology destined to be expressed in a more mature and fruitful manner in the following century, should not be forgotten. Nor should some of his insights be underestimated, such as, for example, his affirmation that non-Christian religious traditions already contain a preparation for the acceptance of Christ, the divine Word.

What can we learn today from the confrontation, frequently in very heated tones, between Bernard and Abelard and, in general, between monastic theology and scholastic theology? First of all I believe that it demonstrates the usefulness and need for healthy theological discussion within the Church, especially when the questions under discussion are not defined by the Magisterium, which nevertheless remains an ineluctable reference point. St. Bernard, but also Abelard himself, always recognized her authority unhesitatingly. Furthermore, Abelard's condemnation on various occasions reminds us that in the theological field there must be a balance between what we may call the architectural principles given to us by Revelation, which therefore always retain their priority importance, and the principles for interpretation suggested by philosophy, that is, by reason, which have an important but exclusively practical role. When this balance between the architecture and the instruments for interpretation is lacking, theological reflection risks being distorted by errors, and it is then the task of the Magisterium to exercise that necessary service to the truth which belongs to it. It must be emphasized in addition that among the reasons that induced Bernard to "take sides" against Abelard and to call for the intervention of the Magisterium, was also his concern to safeguard simple and humble believers, who must be defended when they risk becoming confused or misled by excessively personal opinions or by anticonformist theological argumentation that might endanger their faith.

Lastly, I would like to recall that the theological confrontation between Bernard and Abelard ended with their complete reconciliation, thanks to the mediation of a common friend, Peter the Venerable, the Abbot of Cluny of whom I have spoken in my previous book (*The Fathers, Volume II*). Abelard showed humility in recognizing his errors, Bernard used great benevolence. They both upheld the most important value in a theological controversy: to preserve the Church's faith and to make the truth in charity triumph. Today too may this be the attitude with which we confront one another in the Church, having as our goal the constant quest for truth.

# CHAPTER THREE

# The Cluniac Reform[1]

There was a monastic movement that was very important in the Middle Ages. It is the Order of Cluny, which at the beginning of the twelfth century, at the height of its expansion, had almost 1,200 monasteries: a truly impressive figure! A monastery was founded at Cluny in 910, precisely 1,100 years ago, and subsequent to the donation of William the Pious, Duke of Aquitaine, was placed under the guidance of Abbot Berno. At that time Western monasticism, which had flourished several centuries earlier with St. Benedict, was experiencing a severe decline for various reasons: unstable political and social conditions due to the continuous invasions and sacking by peoples who were not integrated into the fabric of Europe, widespread poverty and, especially, the dependence of abbeys on the local nobles who controlled all that belonged to the territories under their jurisdiction. In this context, Cluny was the heart and soul of a profound renewal of monastic life that led it back to its original inspiration.

At Cluny the Rule of St. Benedict was restored with several adaptations which had already been introduced by other reformers. The main objective was to guarantee the central role that the Liturgy must have in Christian life. The Cluniac monks devoted themselves with love and great care to the celebration of the Liturgical Hours, to the singing of the Psalms, to processions as

---

[1] Pope Benedict XVI, General Audience, November 11, 2009.

devout as they were solemn, and above all, to the celebration of Holy Mass. They promoted sacred music, they wanted architecture and art to contribute to the beauty and solemnity of the rites; they enriched the liturgical calendar with special celebrations such as, for example, at the beginning of November, the Commemoration of All Souls, which we too have just celebrated; and they intensified the devotion to the Virgin Mary. Great importance was given to the Liturgy because the monks of Cluny were convinced that it was participation in the liturgy of Heaven. And the monks felt responsible for interceding at the altar of God for the living and the dead, given large numbers of the faithful were insistently asking them to be remembered in prayer. Moreover, it was with this same aim that William the Pious had desired the foundation of the Abbey of Cluny. In the ancient document that testifies to the foundation we read: "With this gift I establish that a monastery of regulars be built at Cluny in honor of the Holy Apostles Peter and Paul, where monks who live according to the Rule of St. Benedict shall gather ... so that a venerable sanctuary of prayer with vows and supplications may be visited there, and the heavenly life be sought after and yearned for with every desire and with deep ardor, and that assiduous prayers, invocations and supplications be addressed to the Lord."

*Great importance was given to the Liturgy because the monks of Cluny were convinced that it was participation in the liturgy of Heaven.*

To preserve and foster this atmosphere of prayer, the Cluniac Rule emphasized the importance of silence, to which discipline the monks willingly submitted, convinced that the purity of the virtues to which they aspired demanded deep and constant recollection. It is not surprising that before long the Monastery of Cluny gained a reputation for holiness and that many other monastic communities decided to follow its discipline. Numerous princes and Popes asked the abbots of Cluny to extend their reform so that in a short time a dense network of monasteries developed that were linked to Cluny, either by true and proper juridical bonds or by a sort of charismatic affiliation. Thus a spiritual Europe gradually took shape in the various regions of France and in Italy, Spain, Germany, and Hungary.

Cluny's success was assured primarily not only by the lofty spirituality cultivated there but also by several other conditions that ensured its development. In comparison with what had happened until then, the Monastery of Cluny and the communities dependent upon it were recognized as exempt from the jurisdiction of the local bishops and were directly subject to that of the Roman Pontiff. This meant that Cluny had a special bond with the See of Peter and, precisely because of the protection and encouragement of the pontiffs the ideals of purity and fidelity proposed by the Cluniac Reform spread rapidly. Furthermore, the abbots were elected without any interference from the civil authorities, unlike what happened in other places. Truly worthy people succeeded one another at the helm of Cluny and of the numerous monastic communities dependent upon it: Abbot Odo of Cluny, and other great figures such as Eymard, Majolus, Odilo, and especially Hugh the Great, who served for long periods, thereby assuring stability and the spread of the reform embarked upon. As well as Odo, Majolus, Odilo, and Hugh are venerated as saints.

Not only did the Cluniac Reform have positive effects in the purification and reawakening of monastic life but also in the life of the universal Church. In fact, the aspiration to evangelical perfection was an incentive to fight two great abuses that afflicted the Church in that period: simony, that is the acquisition of pastoral offices for money, and immorality among the secular clergy. The abbots of Cluny with their spiritual authority, the Cluniac monks who became bishops and some of them even popes, took the lead in this impressive action of spiritual renewal. And it yielded abundant fruit: celibacy was once again esteemed and practiced by priests, and more transparent procedures were introduced in the designation of ecclesiastical offices.

Also significant were the benefits that monasteries inspired by the Cluniac Reform contributed to society. At a time when Church institutions alone provided for the poor, charity was practiced with dedication. In all the houses, the almoner was bound to offer hospitality to needy wayfarers and pilgrims, travelling priests and religious and especially the poor who came asking for food and a roof over their heads for a few days. Equally important were two other institutions promoted by Cluny that were characteristic of medieval civilization: the "Truce of God" and the "Peace of God." In an epoch heavily marked by violence and the spirit of revenge, with the "Truces of God" long periods of nonbelligerence were guaranteed, especially on the occasion of specific religious feasts and certain days of the week. With "the Peace of God," on pain of a canonical reprimand, respect was requested for defenseless people and for sacred places.

In this way, in the conscience of the peoples of Europe during that long process of gestation, which was to lead to their ever clearer recognition, two fundamental elements for the construction of society matured, namely, the value of the human person and the primary good of peace. Furthermore, as happened for other monastic foundations, the Cluniac monasteries had likewise at their disposal extensive properties which, diligently put to good use, helped to develop the economy. Alongside the manual work there was no lack of the typical cultural activities of medieval monasticism such as schools for children, the foundation of libraries and *scriptoria* for the transcription of books.

In this way, 1,000 years ago when the development of the European identity had gathered momentum, the experience of Cluny, which had spread across vast regions of the European continent, made its important and precious contribution. It recalled the primacy of spiritual benefits; it kept alive the aspiration to the things of God; it inspired and encouraged initiatives and institutions for the promotion of human values; it taught a spirit of peace. Dear brothers and sisters let us pray that all those who have at heart an authentic humanism and the future of Europe may be able to rediscover, appreciate, and defend the rich cultural and religious heritage of these centuries.

# CHAPTER FOUR

# The Cathedral from the Romanesque to the Gothic Architecture: The Theological Background[1]

In previous chapters I have presented several aspects of medieval theology. The Christian faith, however, deeply rooted in the men and women of those centuries, did not only give rise to masterpieces of theological literature, thought, and faith. It also inspired one of the loftiest expressions of universal civilization: the cathedral, the true glory of the Christian Middle Ages. Indeed, for about three centuries, from the beginning of the eleventh century, Europe experienced extraordinary artistic creativity and fervor. An ancient chronicler described the enthusiasm and the hard-working spirit of those times in these words: "It happens that throughout the world, but especially in Italy and in Gaul, people began rebuilding churches although many had no need of such restoration because they were still in good condition. It was like a competition between one people and another; one might have believed that the world, shaking off its rags and tatters, wanted to be reclad throughout in the white mantle of new churches. In short, all these cathedral churches, a large number of monastic churches and even village oratories, were restored by the faithful at that time" (Rodolphus Glaber, *Historiarum*, libri quinque, 3, 4).

---

[1] Pope Benedict, General Audience, November 18, 2009.

Various factors contributed to this rebirth of religious architecture. First of all more favorable historical conditions, such as greater political stability, accompanied by a constant increase in the population and the gradual development of the cities, trade, and wealth. Furthermore, architects found increasingly complicated technical solutions to increase the size of buildings, at the same time guaranteeing them both soundness and majesty. It was mainly thanks to the enthusiasm and spiritual zeal of monasticism, at the height of its expansion, that abbey churches were built in which the Liturgy might be celebrated with dignity and solemnity. They became the destination of continuous pilgrimages where the faithful, attracted by the veneration of saints' relics, could pause in prayer. So it was that the Romanesque churches and cathedrals came into being. They were characterized by the longitudinal development, in length, of the aisles, in order to accommodate numerous faithful. They were very solid churches with thick walls, stone vaults, and simple, spare lines. An innovation was the introduction of sculptures. Because Romanesque churches were places for monastic prayer and for the worship of the faithful, rather than being concerned with technical perfection, the sculptors turned their attention in particular to the educational dimension.

Since it was necessary to inspire in souls strong impressions, sentiments that could persuade them to shun vice and evil and to practice virtue and goodness, the recurrent theme was the portrayal of Christ as Universal Judge surrounded by figures of the Apocalypse. It was usually the portals of the Romanesque churches which displayed these figures, to emphasize that Christ is the Door that leads to Heaven. On crossing the threshold of the sacred building, the faithful entered a space and time different from that of their ordinary life. Within the church, believers in a sovereign, just, and merciful Christ in the artists' intention could enjoy in anticipation eternal beatitude in the celebration of the liturgy and of devotional acts carried out in the sacred building.

In the twelfth and thirteenth centuries another kind of architecture for sacred buildings spread from the north of France: the Gothic. It had two new characteristics in comparison with the Romanesque, a soaring upward movement and luminosity. Gothic cathedrals show a synthesis of faith and art harmoniously expressed in the fascinating universal language of beauty which still elicits wonder today. By the introduction of vaults with pointed arches supported by robust pillars, it was possible to increase their height considerably. The upward thrust was intended as an invitation to prayer and at the same time was itself a prayer. Thus the Gothic cathedral intended to express in its architectural lines the soul's longing for God. In addition, by employing the new technical solutions, it was possible to make openings in the outer walls and to embellish them with stained-glass windows. In other words the windows became great luminous images, very suitable for instructing the people in faith. In them scene by scene the life of a saint, a parable, or some other biblical event were recounted. A cascade of light poured through the stained-glass upon the faithful to tell them the story of salvation and to involve them in this story.

*Thus the Gothic cathedral intended to express in its architectural lines the soul's longing for God.*

Another merit of Gothic cathedrals is that the whole Christian and civil community participated in their building and decoration in harmonious and complementary ways. The lowly and the powerful, the illiterate and the learned; all participated because in this common house all believers were instructed in the faith. Gothic sculpture in fact has made cathedrals into "stone Bibles," depicting Gospel episodes and illustrating the content of the liturgical year, from the Nativity to the glorification of the Lord. In those centuries too, the perception of the Lord's humanity became ever more widespread, and the sufferings of his Passion were represented realistically: the suffering Christ (*Christus patiens*) an image beloved by all and apt to inspire devotion and repentance for sins. Nor were Old Testament figures lacking; thus to the faithful who went to the cathedral their histories became familiar as part of the one common history of salvation. With faces full of beauty, gentleness, and intelligence, Gothic sculpture of the thirteenth century reveals a happy and serene religious sense, glad to show a heartfelt filial devotion to the Mother of God, sometimes seen as a young woman, smiling and motherly, but mainly portrayed as the Queen of Heaven and earth, powerful and merciful.

The faithful who thronged the Gothic cathedrals also liked to find there, expressed in works of art, saints, models of Christian life and intercessors with God. And there was no shortage of the "secular" scenes of life, thus, here and there, there are depictions of work in the fields, of the sciences and arts. All was oriented and offered to God in the place in which the Liturgy was celebrated. We may understand better the meaning attributed to a Gothic cathedral by reflecting on the text of the inscription engraved on the central portal of Saint-Denis in Paris: "Passerby, who is stirred to praise the beauty of these doors, do not let yourself be dazzled by the gold or by the magnificence, but rather by the painstaking work. Here a famous work shines out, but may Heaven deign that this famous work that shines make spirits resplendent so that, with the luminous truth, they may walk toward the true light, where Christ is the true door."

Dear brothers and sisters, I would now like to emphasize two elements of Romanesque and Gothic art that are also helpful to us. The first: the masterpieces of art created in Europe in past centuries are incomprehensible unless one takes into account the religious spirit that inspired them. Marc Chagall, an artist who has always witnessed to the encounter between aesthetics and faith, wrote that "For centuries painters dipped their brushes into that colorful alphabet which was the Bible." When faith, celebrated in the Liturgy in a special way, encounters art, it creates a profound harmony because each can and wishes to speak of God, making the Invisible visible. I would like to share this encounter with artists, renewing to them the proposal of friendship between Christian spirituality and art that my venerable predecessors hoped for, especially the Servants of God Paul VI and John Paul II. The second element: the strength of the Romanesque style and the splendor of the Gothic cathedrals remind us that the *via pulchritudinis*, the way of beauty, is a privileged and fascinating path on which to approach the Mystery of God.

What is the beauty that writers, poets, musicians, and artists contemplate and express in their language other than the reflection of the splendor of the eternal Word made flesh? Then St. Augustine says: "Question the beauty of the earth, question the beauty of the sea, question the beauty of the air, amply spread around everywhere, question the beauty of the sky, question the serried ranks of the stars, question the sun making the day glorious with its bright beams, question the moon tempering the darkness of the following night with its shining rays, question the animals that move in the waters, that amble about on dry land, that fly in the air; their souls hidden, their bodies evident; the visible bodies needing to be controlled, the invisible souls controlling them. Question all these things. They all answer you, 'Here we are, look; we're beautiful!' Their beauty is their confession. Who made these beautiful changeable things, if not one who is beautiful and unchangeable?" (*Sermo* CCXLI, 2: *PL* 38, 1134).

Dear brothers and sisters, may the Lord help us to rediscover the way of beauty as one of the itineraries, perhaps the most attractive and fascinating, on which to succeed in encountering and loving God.

# CHAPTER FIVE

# Hugh and Richard of Saint-Victor[1]

I have presented several exemplary figures of believers who were dedicated to showing the harmony between reason and faith and to witnessing with their lives to the proclamation of the Gospel. Now I intend to write about Hugh and Richard of Saint-Victor. Both were among those philosophers and theologians known as "Victorines" because they lived and taught at the Abbey of Saint-Victor in Paris, founded at the beginning of the twelfth century by William of Champeaux. William himself was a well-known teacher who succeeded in giving his abbey a solid cultural identity. Indeed, a school for the formation of the monks, also open to external students, was founded at Saint-Victor, where a felicitous synthesis was achieved between the two theological models which I have addressed previously. These are monastic theology, primarily oriented to contemplation of the mysteries of the faith in Scripture; and scholastic theology, which aimed to use reason to scrutinize these mysteries with innovative methods in order to create a theological system.

We have little information about the life of Hugh of Saint-Victor. The date and place of his birth are uncertain; he may have been born in Saxony or in Flanders. It is known that having arrived in Paris, the European cultural capital at that time, he spent the rest of his days at the Abbey of Saint-Victor, where he was

---

first a disciple and subsequently a teacher. Even before his death in 1141, he earned great fame and esteem, to the point that he was called a "second St. Augustine." Like Augustine, in fact, he meditated deeply on the relationship between faith and reason, between the secular sciences and theology. According to Hugh of Saint-Victor, in addition to being useful for understanding the Scriptures, all the branches of knowledge have intrinsic value and must be cultivated in order to broaden human knowledge, as well as to answer the human longing to know the truth. This healthy intellectual curiosity led him to counsel students always to give free reign to their desire to learn. In his treatise on the methodology of knowledge and pedagogy, entitled significantly *Didascalicon (On Teaching)* his recommendation was: "Learn willingly what you do not know from everyone. The person who has sought to learn something from everyone will be wiser than them all. The person who receives something from everyone ends by becoming the richest of all" (*Eruditiones Didascalicae,* 3, 14; *PL* 176, 774).

The knowledge with which the philosophers and theologians known as *Victorines* were concerned in particular was theology, which requires first and foremost the loving study of Sacred Scripture. In fact, in order to know God one cannot but begin with what God himself has chosen to reveal of himself in the Scriptures. In this regard Hugh of Saint-Victor is a typical representative of monastic theology, based entirely on biblical exegesis. To interpret Scripture he suggests the traditional patristic and medieval structure, namely, the literal and historical sense first of all, then the allegorical and anagogical and, lastly, the moral. These are four dimensions of the meaning of Scripture that are being rediscovered even today. For this reason one sees that in the text and in the proposed narrative a more profound meaning is concealed: the thread of faith that leads us heavenwards and guides us on this earth, teaching us how to live. Yet, while respecting these four dimensions of the meaning of Scripture, in an original way in comparison with his contemporaries, Hugh of Saint-Victor insists — and this is something new — on the importance of the historical and literal meaning.

In other words before discovering the symbolic value, the deeper dimensions of the biblical text, it is necessary to know and to examine the meaning of the event as it is told in Scripture. Otherwise, he warns, using an effective comparison, one risks being like grammarians who do not know the elementary rules. To those who know the meaning of history as described in the Bible, human events appear marked by divine Providence, in accordance with a clearly ordained plan. Thus, for Hugh of Saint-Victor, history is neither the outcome of a blind destiny nor as meaningless as it might seem. On the contrary, the Holy Spirit is at work in human history and inspires the marvelous dialogue of human beings with God, their friend. This theological view of history highlights the astonishing and salvific intervention of God who truly enters and acts in history. It is almost as if he takes part in our history, while ever preserving and respecting the human being's freedom and responsibility.

Our author considered that the study of Sacred Scripture and its historical and literal meaning makes possible true and proper theology, that is, the systematic illustration of truths, knowledge of their structure, the illustration of the dogmas of the faith. He presents these in a solid synthesis in his Treatise *De Sacramentis Christianae Fidei* (The Sacraments of the Christian Faith). Among other things, he provides a definition of "sacrament" which, further perfected by other theologians, contains ideas that are still very interesting today. "The sacrament is a corporeal or material element proposed in an external and tangible way," he writes, "which by its likeness *makes present* an invisible and spiritual grace; it *signifies* it, because it was instituted to this end, and *contains* it, because it is capable of sanctifying" (9, 2: *PL* 176, 317).

On the one hand is the visibility in the symbol, the "corporeity" of the gift of God. On the other hand, however, in him is concealed the divine grace that comes from the history of Jesus Christ, who himself created the fundamental symbols. Therefore, there are three elements that contribute to the definition of a sacrament, according to Hugh of Saint-Victor: the institution by Christ; the communication of grace; and the analogy between the visible or material element and the invisible element: the divine gifts. This vision is very close to our contemporary understanding, because the sacraments are presented with a language interwoven with symbols and images capable of speaking directly to the human heart. Today too it is important that liturgical animators, and priests in particular, with pastoral wisdom, give due weight to the signs proper to sacramental rites to this visibility and tangibility of Grace. They should pay special attention to catechesis, to ensure that all the faithful experience every celebration of the sacraments with devotion, intensity, and spiritual joy.

Richard, who came from Scotland, was Hugh of Saint-Victor's worthy disciple. He was prior of the Abbey of Saint-Victor from 1162 to 1173, the year of his death. Richard too, of course, assigned a fundamental role to the study of the Bible but, unlike his master, gave priority to the allegorical sense, the symbolic meaning of Scripture. This is what he uses, for example, in his interpretation of the Old Testament figure of Benjamin, the son of Jacob, as a model of contemplation and the epitome of the spiritual life. Richard addresses this topic in two texts, *Benjamin Minor* and *Benjamin Maior*. In these he proposes to the faithful a spiritual journey which is primarily an invitation to exercise the various virtues, learning to discipline and to control with reason the sentiments and the inner affective and emotional impulses. Only when the human being has attained balance and human maturity in this area is he or she ready to approach contemplation, which Richard defines as "a profound and pure gaze of the soul, fixed on the marvels of wisdom, combined with an ecstatic sense of wonder and admiration" (*Benjamin Maior* 1, 4: *PL* 196, 67).

Contemplation is therefore the destination, the result of an arduous journey that involves dialogue between faith and reason, that is once again a theological discourse. Theology stems from truths that are the subject of faith but seeks to deepen knowledge of them by the use of reason, taking into account the gift of faith. This application of reason to the comprehension of faith is presented convincingly in Richard's masterpiece, one of the great books of history, the *De Trinitate* (*The Trinity*). In the six volumes of which it is composed he reflects perspicaciously on the Mystery of the Triune God. According to our author, since God is love, the one divine substance includes communication, oblation, and love between the two Persons, the Father and the Son, who are placed in a reciprocal, eternal exchange of love. However, the perfection of happiness and goodness admits of no exclusivism or closure. On the contrary, it requires the eternal presence of a third Person, the Holy Spirit. Trinitarian love is participatory, harmonious, and includes a superabundance of delight, enjoyment, and ceaseless joy. Richard, in other words, supposes that God is love; analyzes the essence of love, of what the reality love entails; and thereby arrives at the Trinity of the Persons, which really is the logical expression of the fact that God is love.

Yet Richard is aware that love, although it reveals to us the essence of God, although it makes us "understand" the Mystery

> *Theology stems from truths that are the subject of faith but seeks to deepen knowledge of them by the use of reason, taking into account the gift of faith.*

of the Trinity, is nevertheless always an analogy that serves to speak of a Mystery that surpasses the human mind. Being the poet and mystic that he is, Richard also has recourse to other images. For example, he compares divinity to a river, to a loving wave which originates in the Father and ebbs and flows in the Son, to be subsequently spread with joy through the Holy Spirit.

Dear friends, authors such as Hugh and Richard of Saint-Victor raise our minds to contemplation of the divine realities. At the same time, the immense joy we feel at the thought, admiration and praise of the Blessed Trinity supports and sustains the practical commitment to be inspired by this perfect model of communion in love in order to build our daily human relationships. The Trinity is truly perfect communion! How the world would change if relations were always lived in families, in parishes, and in every other community by following the example of the three divine Persons in whom each lives not only *with* the other, but *for* the other and *in* the other! At the Angelus on June 7, 2009, I recalled: "Love alone makes us happy because we live in a relationship, and we live to love and to be loved." It is love that works this ceaseless miracle. As in the life of the Blessed Trinity, plurality is recomposed in unity, where all is kindness and joy. With St. Augustine, held in great honor by the *Victorines,* we too may exclaim: "*Vides Trinitatem, si caritatem vides* — you contemplate the Trinity, if you see charity" (*De Trinitate* VIII, 8, 12).

# CHAPTER SIX

# William of Saint-Thierry[1]

Bernard of Clairvaux, the "Doctor Mellifluus," was a great protagonist of the twelfth century. His biographer, a friend who esteemed him, was William of Saint-Thierry on whom I now reflect.

William was born in Liège between 1075 and 1080. He came from a noble family, was endowed with a keen intelligence and an innate love of study. He attended famous schools of the time, such as those in his native city and in Rheims, France. He also came into personal contact with Abelard, the teacher who applied philosophy to theology in such an original way as to give rise to great perplexity and opposition. William also expressed his own reservations, pressing his friend Bernard to take a stance concerning Abelard. Responding to God's mysterious and irresistible call which is the vocation to the consecrated life, William entered the Benedictine Monastery of Saint-Nicasius in Rheims in 1113. A few years later he became abbot of the Monastery of Saint-Thierry in the Diocese of Rheims. In that period there was a widespread need for the purification and renewal of monastic life to make it authentically evangelical. William worked on doing this in his own monastery and in general in the Benedictine Order. However, he met with great resistance to his attempts at reform and thus, although his friend Bernard advised him against

---

[1] Pope Benedict XVI, General Audience, December 2, 2009.

it, in 1135 he left the Benedictine abbey and exchanged his black habit for a white one in order to join the Cistercians of Signy. From that time, until his death in 1148, he devoted himself to prayerful contemplation of God's mysteries, ever the subject of his deepest desires, and to the composition of spiritual literature, important writings in the history of monastic theology.

One of his first works is entitled *De Natura et dignitate amoris (The nature and dignity of love)*. In it William expressed one of his basic ideas that is also valid for us. The principal energy that moves the human soul, he said, is love. Human nature, in its deepest essence, consists in loving. Ultimately, a single task is entrusted to every human being: to learn to like and to love, sincerely, authentically and freely. However, it is only from God's teaching that this task is learned and that the human being may reach the end for which he was created. Indeed, William wrote: "The art of arts is the art of love.... Love is inspired by the Creator of nature. Love is a force of the soul that leads it as by a natural weight to its own place and end" (*De Natura et dignitate amoris* 1 *PL* 184, 379). Learning to love is a long and demanding process that is structured by William in four stages, corresponding to the ages of the human being: childhood, youth, maturity, and old age. On this journey the person must impose upon himself an effective ascesis, firm self-control to eliminate every irregular affection, every capitulation to selfishness, and to unify his own life in God, the source, goal, and force of love, until he reaches the summit of spiritual life which William calls "wisdom." At the end of this ascetic process, the person feels deep serenity and sweetness. All the human being's faculties — intelligence, will, affection — rest in God, known and loved in Christ.

In other works too, William speaks of this radical vocation to love for God which is the secret of a successful and happy life and which he describes as a ceaseless, growing desire, inspired by

God himself in the human heart. In a meditation he says "that the object of this love is Love" with a capital "L" — namely, God. It is he who pours himself out into the hearts of those who love him and prepares them to receive him. "God gives himself until the person is sated and in such a way that the desire is never lacking. This impetus of love is the fulfillment of the human being" (*De Contemplando Deo* 6, *passim, SC* 61 bis, pp. 79–83). The considerable importance that William gives to the emotional dimension is striking. Basically, dear friends, our hearts are made of flesh and blood, and when we love God, who is Love itself, how can we fail to express in this relationship with the Lord our most human feelings, such as tenderness, sensitivity, and delicacy? In becoming Man, the Lord himself wanted to love us with a heart of flesh!

Moreover, according to William, love has another important quality: it illuminates the mind and enables one to know God better and more profoundly and, in God, people and events. The knowledge that proceeds from the senses and the intelligence reduces but does not eliminate the distance between the subject and the object, between the "I" and the "you." Love, on the other hand, gives rise to attraction and communion, to the point that transformation and assimilation take place between the subject who loves and the beloved object. This reciprocity of affection and liking subsequently permits a far deeper knowledge than that which is brought by reason alone. A famous saying of William expresses it: "*Amor ipse intellectus est* — love in itself is already the beginning of knowledge." Dear friends, let us ask ourselves: is not our life just like this? Is it not perhaps true that we only truly know *who* and *what* we love? Without a certain fondness one knows no one and nothing! And this applies first of all to the knowledge of God and his mysteries that exceed our mental capacity to understand: God is known if he is loved!

A synthesis of William of Saint-Thierry's thought is contained in a long letter addressed to the Carthusians of Mont-Dieu, whom he visited and wished to encourage and console.

*One therefore arrives at the perfection of spiritual life when the realities of faith are a source of deep joy and real and satisfying communion with God.*

Already in 1690, the learned Benedictine Jean Mabillon, gave this letter a meaningful title: *Epistola Aurea (Golden Epistle)*. In fact, the teachings on spiritual life that it contains are invaluable for all those who wish to increase in communion with God and in holiness. In this treatise, William proposes an itinerary in three stages. It is necessary, he says, to move on from the "animal" being to the "rational" one, in order to attain to the "spiritual." What does our author mean by these three terms? To start with, a person accepts the vision of life inspired by faith with an act of obedience and trust. Then, with a process of interiorization, in which the reason and the will play an important role, faith in Christ is received with profound conviction and one feels a harmonious correspondence between what is believed and what is hoped, and the most secret aspirations of the soul, our reason, our affections. One therefore arrives at the perfection of spiritual life when the realities of faith are a source of deep joy and real and satisfying communion with God. One lives only in love and for love. William based this process on a solid vision of the human being inspired by the ancient Greek Fathers, especially Origen who, with bold language, taught that the human being's vocation was to become like God who created him in his image and likeness.

The image of God present in man impels him toward likeness, that is, toward an ever fuller identity between his own will and the divine will. One does not attain this perfection, which

William calls "unity of spirit," by one's own efforts, even if they are sincere and generous, because something else is necessary. This perfection is reached through the action of the Holy Spirit who takes up his abode in the soul and purifies, absorbs, and transforms into charity every impulse and desire of love that is present in the human being. "Then there is a further likeness to God," we read in the *Epistola Aurea*, "which is no longer called 'likeness' but 'unity of spirit,' when the person becomes one with God, one in spirit, not only because of the unity of an identical desire but through being unable to desire anything else. In this way the human being deserves to become not God but what God is: man becomes through grace what God is by nature" (*Epistola Aurea* 262–263, *SC* 223, pp. 353–355).

Dear brothers and sisters, this author, whom we might describe as the "Singer of Charity, of Love," teaches us to make the basic decision in our lives which gives meaning and value to all our other decisions: to love God and, through love of him, to love our neighbor; only in this manner shall we be able to find true joy, an anticipation of eternal beatitude. Let us therefore learn from the saints in order to learn to love authentically and totally, to set our being on this journey. Together with a young saint, a Doctor of the Church, Thérèse of the Child Jesus, let us tell the Lord that we too want to live of love. And I conclude this chapter with a prayer precisely by this saint: "You know I love you, Jesus Christ, my Own! Your Spirit's fire of love enkindles me. By loving you, I draw the Father here, down to my heart, to stay with me always. Blessed Trinity! You are my prisoner dear, of love, today.... To live of love, 'tis without stint to give. And never count the cost, nor ask reward.... O Heart Divine, o'erflowing with tenderness, How swift I run, who all to You has given! Naught but your love I need, my life to bless" [To live of love].

# CHAPTER SEVEN

# Rupert of Deutz[1]

In this chapter we become acquainted with another twelfth-century Benedictine monk. His name is Rupert of Deutz, a city near Cologne, home to a famous monastery. Rupert himself speaks of his own life in one of his most important works entitled *The Glory and Honor of the Son of Man* [*De gloria et honore filii hominis super Matthaeum*], which is a commentary on part of the Gospel according to Matthew. While still a boy he was received at the Benedictine Monastery of St. Laurence at Liège as an "oblate," in accordance with the custom at that time of entrusting one of the sons to the monks for his education, intending to make him a gift to God. Rupert always loved monastic life. He quickly learned Latin in order to study the Bible and to enjoy the liturgical celebrations. He distinguished himself for his moral rectitude, straight as a die, and his strong attachment to the See of St. Peter.

Rupert's time was marked by disputes between the Papacy and the Empire, because of the so-called "Investiture Controversy" with which, as I have mentioned previously, the Papacy wished to prevent the appointment of bishops and the exercise of their jurisdiction from depending on the civil authorities who were certainly not guided by pastoral reasons but for the most part by political and financial considerations. Bishop Otbert of

---

[1] Pope Benedict XVI, General Audience, December 9, 2009.

Liège resisted the Pope's directives and exiled Berengarius, Abbot of the Monastery of St. Laurence, because of his fidelity to the Pontiff. It was in this monastery that Rupert lived. He did not hesitate to follow his Abbot into exile, and only when Bishop Otbert returned to communion with the Pope did he return to Liège and agree to become a priest. Until that moment, in fact, he had avoided receiving ordination from a bishop in dissent with the pope. Rupert teaches us that when controversies arise in the Church the reference to the Petrine ministry guarantees fidelity to sound doctrine and is a source of serenity and inner freedom. After the dispute with Otbert Rupert was obliged to leave his monastery again twice. In 1116 his adversaries even wanted to take him to court. Although he was acquitted of every accusation, Rupert preferred to go for a while to Siegburg; but since on his return to the monastery in Liège the disputes had not yet ceased, he decided to settle definitively in Germany. In 1120 he was appointed Abbot of Deutz where, except for making a pilgrimage to Rome in 1124, he lived until 1129, the year of his death.

A fertile writer, Rupert left numerous works, still today of great interest because he played an active part in various important theological discussions of his time. For example, he intervened with determination in the Eucharistic controversy, which in 1077 led to his condemnation by Berengarius of Tours. Berengarius had given a reductive interpretation of Christ's presence in the Sacrament of the Eucharist, describing it as merely symbolic. In the language of the Church the term "transubstantiation" was as yet unknown, but Rupert, at times with daring words, made himself a staunch supporter of the Eucharistic reality and, es-

*Rupert teaches us that when controversies arise in the Church the reference to the Petrine ministry guarantees fidelity to sound doctrine and is a source of serenity and inner freedom.*

pecially in a work entitled *De divinis officiis* (On divine offices), purposefully asserted the continuity between the Body of the Incarnate Word of Christ and that present in the Eucharistic species of the bread and the wine.

Dear brothers and sisters, it seems to me that at this point we must also think of our time; today too we are in danger of reappraising the Eucharistic reality, that is, of considering the Eucharist almost as a rite of communion, of socialization alone, forgetting all too easily that the Risen Christ is really present in the Eucharist with his Risen Body which is placed in our hands *to draw us out* of ourselves, *to incorporate us* into his immortal body and thereby *lead us* to new life. This great mystery that the Lord is present in his full reality in the Eucharistic species is a mystery to be adored and loved ever anew! I would like here to quote the words of the *Catechism of the Catholic Church* which bear the fruit of 2,000 years of meditation on the faith and theological reflection: "The mode of Christ's presence under the Eucharistic species is unique and incomparable.... In the most blessed sacrament of the Eucharist 'the Body and Blood, together with the soul and divinity, of our Lord Jesus Christ ... is truly, really, and substantially contained.' ... It is a substantial presence by which Christ, God and man, makes himself wholly and entirely present ... by the Eucharistic species of the bread the wine" (cf. n. 1374). Rupert too contributed with his reflections to this precise formulation.

Another controversy in which the Abbot of Deutz was involved concerns the problem of the reconciliation of God's goodness and omnipotence with the existence of evil. If God is omnipotent and good, how is it possible to explain the reality of evil? Rupert, in fact, reacted to the position assumed by the teachers of the theological school of Laon, who, with a series of philosophical arguments, distinguished in God's will the "to approve" and the "to permit," concluding that God permits evil without approving it and hence without desiring it. Rupert, on the other hand, renounces the use of philosophy, which he deems inadequate for addressing such a great problem, and remains simply faithful to the biblical narration. He starts with the goodness of God, with the truth that God is supremely good and cannot desire anything but good. Thus he identifies the origin of evil in the human being himself and in the erroneous use of human freedom. When Rupert addresses this topic, he writes pages filled with religious inspiration to praise the Father's infinite mercy, God's patience with the sinful human being and his kindness to him.

Like other medieval theologians, Rupert too wondered why the Word of God, the Son of God, was made man. Some, many, answered by explaining the Incarnation of the Word by the urgent need to atone for human sin. Rupert, on the other hand, with a Christocentric vision of salvation history, broadens the perspective, and in a work entitled *The Glorification of the Trinity,* sustains the position that the Incarnation, the central event of the whole of history was planned from eternity, even independently of human sin, so that the whole creation might praise God the Father and love him as one family gathered round Christ, the Son of God. Then he saw in the pregnant woman of the Apocalypse the entire history of humanity which is oriented to Christ, just as conception is oriented to birth, a perspective that was to be developed by other thinkers and enhanced by contemporary theology, which says that the whole history of the world and of humanity is a conception oriented to the birth of Christ. Christ is always the center of the exegetic explanations provided by Rupert in his commentaries on the Books of the Bible, to which he dedicated himself with great diligence and passion. Thus, he rediscovers a wonderful unity in all the events of the history of salvation, from the creation until the final consummation of time: "All Scripture," he says, "is one book, which aspires to the same end (the divine Word); which comes from one God and was written by one Spirit" (*De glorificatione Trinitatis et procesione Sancti spiritus* I, V, *PL* 169, 18).

In the interpretation of the Bible, Rupert did not limit himself to repeating the teaching of the Fathers, but shows an originality of his own. For example, he is the first writer to have identified the bride in the Song of Songs with Mary Most Holy. His commentary on this book of Scripture has thus turned out to be a sort of Mariological *summa*, in which he presents Mary's privileges and excellent virtues. In one of the most inspired passages of his commentary Rupert writes: "O most beloved among the beloved, Virgin of virgins, what does your beloved Son so praise in you that the whole choir of angels exalts? What they praise is your simplicity, purity, innocence, doctrine, modesty, humility, integrity of mind and body, that is, your incorrupt virginity" (*In Canticum Canticorum* 4, 1–6, *CCL* 26, pp. 69–70). The Marian interpretation of Rupert's *Canticum* is a felicitous example of harmony between liturgy and theology. In fact, various passages of this Book of the Bible were already used in liturgical celebrations on Marian feasts.

Rupert, furthermore, was careful to insert his Mariological doctrine into that ecclesiological doctrine. That is to say, he saw in Mary Most Holy the holiest part of the whole Church. For this reason my venerable predecessor, Pope Paul VI, in his Discourse for the closure of the third session of the Second Vatican Council, in solemnly pronouncing Mary Mother of the Church, even cited a proposal taken from Rupert's works, which describes Mary as *portio maxima, portio optima,* the most sublime part, the very best part of the Church (cf. *In Apocalypsem* 1, 7, *PL* 169, 1043).

Dear friends, from these rapid allusions we realize that Rupert was a fervent theologian endowed with great depth. Like all the representatives of monastic theology, he was able to combine rational study of the mysteries of faith with prayer and contemplation, which he considered the summit of all knowledge of God. He himself sometimes speaks of his mystical experiences, such as when he confides his ineffable joy at having perceived the Lord's presence: "in that brief moment," he says, "I experienced how true what he himself says is. *Learn from me for I am meek and humble of heart"* (*De gloria et honore Filii hominis. Super Matthaeum* 12, *PL* 1168, 1601). We too, each one of us in our own way, can encounter the Lord Jesus who ceaselessly accompanies us on our way, makes himself present in the Eucharistic Bread and in his Word for our salvation.

# CHAPTER EIGHT

# John of Salisbury[1]

In this chapter we shall become acquainted with John of Salisbury who belonged to one of the most important schools of philosophy and theology of the Middle Ages, that of the Cathedral of Chartres in France. Like the theologians of whom I have addressed in previous chapters, John too helps us understand that faith, in harmony with the just aspirations of reason, impels thought toward the revealed truth in which is found the true good of the human being.

John was born in Salisbury, England, between 1100 and 1120. In reading his works, and especially the large collection of his letters, we learn about the most important events in his life. For about 12 years, from 1136 to 1148, he devoted himself to study, attending the best schools of his day where he heard the lectures of famous teachers. He went to Paris and then to Chartres, the environment that made the greatest impression on his formation and from which he assimilated his great cultural openness, his interest in speculative problems and his appreciation of literature. As often happened in that time, the most brilliant students were chosen by prelates and sovereigns to be their close collaborators. This also happened to John of Salisbury, who was introduced to Theobald, Archbishop of Canterbury the Primatial See of England by a great friend of his, Bernard of Clairvaux. Theobald was glad to welcome John among his clergy.

---

[1] Pope Benedict XVI, General Audience, December 16, 2009.

For eleven years, from 1150 to 1161, John was the secretary and chaplain of the elderly Archbishop. With unflagging zeal he continued to devote himself to study; he carried out an intense diplomatic activity, going to Italy ten times for the explicit purpose of fostering relations between the Kingdom and Church of England and the Roman Pontiff. Among other things, the Pope in those years was Adrian IV, an Englishman who was a close friend of John of Salisbury. In the years following Adrian IV's death, in 1159, a situation of serious tension arose in England, between the Church and the Kingdom. In fact, King Henry II wished to impose his authority on the internal life of the Church, curtailing her freedom. This stance provoked John of Salisbury to react and, in particular, prompted the valiant resistance of St. Thomas Becket, Theobald's successor on the episcopal throne of Canterbury, who for this reason was exiled to France. John of Salisbury accompanied him and remained in his service, working ceaselessly for reconciliation. In 1170, when both John and Thomas Becket had returned to England, Thomas was attacked and murdered in his cathedral. He died a martyr and was immediately venerated as such by the people. John continued to serve faithfully the successor of Thomas as well, until he was appointed Bishop of Chartres where he lived from 1176 until 1180, the year of his death.

I would like to point out two of John of Salisbury's works that are considered his masterpieces, bearing elegant Greek titles: *Metalogicon* (In Defense of Logic), and *Policraticus* (The Man of Government). In the first of these works, not without that fine irony that is a feature of many scholars, he rejects the position of those who had a reductionist conception of culture, which they saw as empty eloquence and vain words. John, on the contrary, praises culture, authentic philosophy, that is, the encounter between rigorous thought and communication, effective words.

He writes: "Indeed, just as eloquence that is not illuminated by reason is not only rash but blind, so wisdom that does not profit from the use of words is not only weak but in a certain way is mutilated. Indeed, although, at times, wisdom without words might serve to square the individual with his own conscience, it is of rare or little profit to society" (*Metalogicon,* 1, 1, *PL* 199, 327). This is a very timely teaching. Today, what John described as "eloquence," that is, the possibility of communicating with increasingly elaborate and widespread means, has increased enormously. Yet the need to communicate messages endowed with "wisdom," that is inspired by truth, goodness, and beauty, is more urgent than ever. This is a great responsibility that calls into question in particular the people who work in the multiform and complex world of culture, of communications, of the *media.* And this is a realm in which the Gospel can be proclaimed with missionary zeal.

In the *Metalogicon* John treats the problems of logic, in his day a subject of great interest, and asks himself a fundamental question: what can human reason know? To what point can it correspond with the aspiration that exists in every person, namely, to seek the truth? John of Salisbury adopts a moderate position, based on the teaching of certain treatises of Aristotle and Cicero. In his opinion human reason normally attains knowledge that is not indisputable but probable and arguable. Human knowledge — this is his conclusion — is imperfect, because it is subject to finiteness, to human limitations. Nevertheless it grows and is perfected, thanks to the experience and elaboration of correct and consistent reasoning, able to make connections between concepts and the reality, through discussion, exchanges, and knowledge that is enriched from one generation to the next. Only in God is there perfect knowledge, which is communicated to the human being, at least partially, by means of Revelation received in faith, which is why the knowledge of faith, theology, unfolds the potential of reason and makes it possible to advance with humility in the knowledge of God's mysteries.

The believer and the theologian who deepen the treasure of faith, also open themselves to a practical knowledge that guides our daily activity, in other words moral law and the exercise of the virtues. John of Salisbury writes: "God's clemency has grant-ed us his law, which establishes what it is useful for us to know and points out to us what it is legitimate for us to know of God and what it is right to investigate.... In this law, in fact, the will of God is explained and revealed so that each one of us may know what he needs to do" (*Metalogicon* 4, 41, *PL* 199, 944–945). Ac-cording to John of Salisbury an immutable objective truth also exists, whose origin is in God, accessible to human reason, and which concerns practical and social action. It is a natural law that must inspire human laws and political and religious authorities, so that they may promote the common good. This natural law is characterized by a property that John calls "equity," that is, the attribution to each person of his own rights. From this stem pre-cepts that are legitimate for all peoples, and in no way can they be abrogated. This is the central thesis of *Policraticus,* the treatise of philosophy and political theology in which John of Salisbury reflects on the conditions that render government leaders just and acceptable.

Whereas other arguments addressed in this work are linked to the historical circumstances in which it was composed, the theme of the relationship between natural law and a positive juridical order, mediated by equity, is still of great importance today. In our time, in fact, especially in some countries, we are witnessing a disturbing divergence between reason, whose task is to discover the ethical values linked to the dignity of the hu-man person, and freedom, whose responsibility is to accept and promote them. Perhaps John of Salisbury would remind us today that the only laws in conformity with equity are those that protect the sacredness of human life and reject the licitness of abortion, euthanasia, and bold genetic experimentation; those laws that respect the dignity of marriage between a man and a woman, that are inspired by a correct secularism of the State, a secularism that always entails the safeguard of religious freedom, and that pursue subsidiarity and solidarity at both the national and the international level. If this were not so, what John of Salisbury terms the "tyranny of princes," or as we would say, "the dictatorship of relativism" would end by coming to power, a relativism, as I recalled a few years ago, "which does not recognize anything as definitive and whose ultimate goal consists solely of one's own ego and desires" (Cardinal Joseph Ratzinger, Dean of the College of Cardinals, *Homily, Mass for the Election of the Roman Pontiff,* April 18, 2005).

*In our time, in fact, especially in some countries, we are witnessing a disturbing divergence between reason, whose task is to discover the ethical values linked to the dignity of the human person, and freedom, whose responsibility is to accept and promote them.*

In my Encyclical, *Caritas in Veritate,* in addressing people of goodwill who strive to ensure that social and political action are never separated from the objective truth about man and his dignity, I wrote: "Truth, and the love which it reveals, cannot be produced: they can only be received as a gift. Their ultimate source is not, and cannot be, mankind, but only God, who is himself Truth and Love. This principle is extremely important for society and for development, since neither can be a purely human product; the vocation to development on the part of individuals and peoples is not based simply on human choice, but is an intrinsic part of a plan that is prior to us and constitutes for all of us a duty to be freely accepted" (n. 52). We must seek and welcome this plan that precedes us, this truth of being, so that justice may be born, but we may find it and welcome it only with a heart, a will, and a reason purified in the light of God.

# CHAPTER NINE

# Peter Lombard[1]

In this chapter I would like to speak about Peter Lombard: he was a theologian who lived in the twelfth century and enjoyed great fame because one of his works, entitled the *Sentences*, was used as a theological manual for many centuries.

So who was Peter Lombard? Although the information on his life is scarce, it is possible to reconstruct the essential lines of his biography. He was born between the eleventh and twelfth centuries near Novara, in Northern Italy, in a region that once belonged to the Lombards. For this very reason he was nicknamed "the Lombard." He belonged to a modest family, as we may deduce from the letter of introduction that Bernard of Clairvaux wrote to Gilduin, Superior of the Abbey of Saint-Victor in Paris, asking him to give free accommodation to Peter who wanted to go to that city in order to study. In fact, even in the Middle Ages not only nobles or the rich might study and acquire important roles in ecclesial and social life but also people of humble origin such as, for example, Gregory VII, the pope who stood up to the Emperor Henry VI, or Maurice of Sully, the Archbishop of Paris who commissioned the building of Notre Dame and who was the son of a poor peasant.

Peter Lombard began his studies in Bologna and then went to Rheims and lastly to Paris. From 1140 he taught at the prestigious

---

[1] Pope Benedict XVI, General Audience, December 30, 2009.

school of Notre Dame. Esteemed and appreciated as a theologian, eight years later he was charged by Pope Eugene II to examine the doctrine of Gilbert de la Porrée that was giving rise to numerous discussions because it was held to be not wholly orthodox. Having become a priest, he was appointed Bishop of Paris in 1159, a year before his death in 1160.

Like all theology teachers of his time, Peter also wrote discourses and commentaries on Sacred Scripture. His masterpiece, however, consists of the four Books of the *Sentences*. This is a text which came into being for didactic purposes. According to the theological method in use in those times, it was necessary first of all to know, study, and comment on the thought of the Fathers of the Church and of the other writers deemed authoritative. Peter therefore collected a very considerable amount of documentation, which consisted mainly of the teachings of the great Latin Fathers, especially St. Augustine, and was open to the contribution of contemporary theologians. Among other things, he also used an encyclopedia of Greek theology which had only recently become known to the West: *The Orthodox Faith*, composed by St. John Damascene.

The great merit of Peter Lombard is to have organized all the material that he had collected and chosen with care, in a systematic and harmonious framework. In fact one of the features of theology is to organize the patrimony of faith in a unitive and orderly way. Thus he distributed the sentences, that is, the Patristic sources on various arguments, in four books. In the first book he addresses God and the Trinitarian mystery; in the second, the work of the Creation, sin and Grace; in the third, the Mystery of the Incarnation and the work of Redemption with an extensive exposition on the virtues. The fourth book is dedicated to the sacraments and to the last realities, those of eternal life, or *Novissimi*. The overall view presented includes almost all the truths of the Catholic faith. The concise, clear vision and clear, orderly schematic and ever consistent presentation explain the extraordinary success of Peter Lombard's *Sentences.* They enabled students to learn reliably and gave the educators and teachers who used them plenty of room for acquiring deeper knowledge. A Franciscan theologian, Alexandre of Hales, of the next generation, introduced into the *Sentences* a division that facilitated their study and consultation. Even the greatest of the thirteenth-century theologians — Albert the Great, Bonaventure of Bagnoregio, and Thomas Aquinas — began their academic activity by commenting on the four books of Peter Lombard's *Sentences,* enriching them with their reflections. Lombard's text was the book in use at all schools of theology until the sixteenth century.

I would like to emphasize how the organic presentation of faith is an indispensable requirement. In fact, the individual truths of faith illuminate each other and, in their total and unitive vision appears the harmony of God's plan of salvation and the centrality of the Mystery of Christ. After the example of Peter Lombard, I invite all theologians and priests always to keep in mind the whole vision of the Christian doctrine, to counter today's risks of fragmentation and the debasement of the single truths. The *Catechism of the Catholic Church,* as well as the *Compendium* of this same Catechism, offer us exactly this full picture of Christian Revelation, to be accepted with faith and gratitude. However I would like to encourage the individual faithful and the Christian communities to make the most of these instruments to know and to deepen the content of our faith. It will thus appear to us as a marvelous symphony that speaks to us of God and of his love and asks of us firm adherence and an active response.

To get an idea of the interest that the reading of Peter Lombard's *Sentences* still inspires today, I propose two examples. Inspired by St. Augustine's Commentary on the Book of Genesis, Peter wonders why woman was created from man's rib and not from his head or his feet. And Peter explains: "She was formed neither as a dominator nor a slave of man but rather as his companion" (*Sentences* 3, 18, 3). Then, still on the basis of the Patristic teaching he adds: "The mystery of Christ and of the Church is represented in this act. Just as, in fact, woman was formed from Adam's rib while he slept, so the Church was born from the sacraments that began to flow from the side of Christ, asleep on the Cross, that is, from the blood and water with which we are redeemed from sin and cleansed of guilt" (*Sentences* 3, 18, 4). These are profound reflections that still apply today when the theology and spirituality of Christian marriage have considerably deepened the analogy with the spousal relationship of Christ and his Church.

In another passage in one of his principal works, Peter Lombard, treating the merits of Christ, asks himself: "Why, then does [Christ] wish to suffer and die, if his virtues were sufficient to obtain for himself all the merits?" His answer is incisive and effective: "For you, not for himself." He then continues with another question and another answer, which seem to reproduce the discussions that went on during the lessons of medieval theology teachers: "And in what sense did he suffer and die for me? So that his Passion and his death might be an example and cause for you. An example of virtue and humility, a cause of glory and freedom; an example given by God, obedient unto death; a cause of your liberation and your beatitude" (*Sentences* 3, 18, 5).

Among the most important contributions offered by Peter Lombard to the history of theology, I would like to recall his treatise on the sacraments, of which he gave what I would call a definitive definition: "precisely what is a sign of God's grace and a visible form of invisible grace, in such a way that it bears its image and is its cause is called a sacrament in the proper sense" (4, 1, 4). With this definition Peter Lombard grasps the essence of the sacraments: they are a cause of grace, they are truly able to communicate divine life. Successive theologians never again departed from this vision and were also to use the distinction between the material and the formal element introduced by the "Master of the Sentences," as Peter Lombard was known. The material element is the tangible visible reality, the formal element consists of the words spoken by the minister. For a complete and valid celebra-

> *Peter Lombard grasps the essence of the sacraments: they are a cause of grace, they are truly able to communicate divine life.*

tion of the sacraments both are essential: matter, the reality with which the Lord visibly touches us, and the word that conveys the spiritual significance. In Baptism, for example, the material element is the water that is poured on the head of the child, and the formal element is the formula: "I baptize you in the name of the Father, of the Son and of the Holy Spirit." Peter the Lombard, moreover, explained that the sacraments alone objectively transmit divine grace and they are seven: Baptism, Confirmation, the Eucharist, Penance, the Unction of the sick, Orders, and Matrimony (cf. *Sentences* 4, 2, 1).

Dear Brothers and Sisters, it is important to recognize how precious and indispensable for every Christian is the sacramental life in which the Lord transmits this matter in the community of the Church, and touches and transforms us. As the *Catechism of the Catholic Church* says, the sacraments are "powers that come forth from the Body of Christ, which is ever-living and life-giving. They are actions of the Holy Spirit" (n. 1116). I urge priests, especially ministers in charge of souls, to have an intense sacramental life themselves in the first place in order to be of help to the faithful. May the celebration of the sacraments be impressed with dignity and decorum, encourage personal recollection and community participation, the sense of God's presence and missionary zeal. The sacraments are the great treasure of the Church, and it is the task of each one of us to celebrate them with spiritual profit. In them an ever-amazing event touches our lives: Christ, through the visible signs, comes to us, purifies us, transforms us, and makes us share in his divine friendship.

# CHAPTER TEN

# The Mendicant Orders[1]

Let us look at the history of Christianity, to see how history develops and how it can be renewed. It shows that saints, guided by God's light, are the authentic reformers of the life of the Church and of society. As teachers with their words and witnesses with their example, they can encourage a stable and profound ecclesial renewal because they themselves are profoundly renewed, they are in touch with the real newness: God's presence in the world. This comforting reality — namely, that in every generation saints are born and bring the creativity of renewal — constantly accompanies the Church's history in the midst of the sorrows and negative aspects she encounters on her path. Indeed, century after century, we also see the birth of forces of reform and renewal, because God's newness is inexhaustible and provides ever new strength to forge ahead. This also happened in the thirteenth century with the birth and the extraordinary development of the Mendicant Orders: an important model of renewal in a new historical epoch. They were given this name because of their characteristic feature of "begging," in other words humbly turning to the people for financial support in order to live their vow of poverty and carry out their evangelizing mission. The best known and most important of the Mendicant Orders that came into being in this period are the Friars Minor

---

[1] Pope Benedict XVI, General Audience, January 13, 2010.

and the Friars Preachers, known as Franciscans and Dominicans. Thus they are called by the names of their Founders, respectively Francis of Assisi and Dominic de Guzmán. These two great saints were able to read "the signs of the times" intelligently, perceiving the challenges that the Church of their time would be obliged to face.

A first challenge was the expansion of various groups and movements of the faithful who, in spite of being inspired by a legitimate desire for authentic Christian life often set themselves outside ecclesial communion. They were profoundly adverse to the rich and beautiful Church which had developed precisely with the flourishing of monasticism. In a previous chapter I reflected on the monastic community of Cluny, which had always attracted young people, therefore vital forces, as well as property and riches. Thus, at the first stage, logically, a Church developed whose wealth was in property and also in buildings. The idea that Christ came down to earth poor and that the true Church must be the very Church of the poor clashed with this Church. The desire for true Christian authenticity was thus in contrast to the reality of the empirical Church. These were the so-called paupers' movements of the Middle Ages. They fiercely contested the way of life of the priests and monks of the time, accused of betraying the Gospel and of not practicing poverty like the early Christians, and these movements countered the Bishops' ministry with their own "parallel hierarchy." Furthermore, to justify their decisions, they disseminated doctrine incompatible with the Catholic faith. For example, the Cathars' or Albigensians' movement re-proposed ancient heresies such as the debasement of and contempt for the material world; the opposition to wealth soon became opposition to material reality as such, the denial of free will and, subsequently, dualism, the existence of a second principle of evil equivalent to God. These movements gained ground, especially in France and Italy, not only because of their solid organization but also because they were denouncing a real disorder in the Church, caused by the far from exemplary behavior of some members of the clergy.

Both Franciscans and Dominicans, following in their Founders' footsteps, showed on the contrary that it was possible to live evangelical poverty, the truth of the Gospel as such, without being separated from the Church. They showed that the Church remains the true, authentic home of the Gospel and of Scripture. Indeed, Dominic and Francis drew the power of their witness precisely from close communion with the Church and the Papacy. With an entirely original decision in the history of consecrated life the members of these Orders not only gave up their personal possessions, as monks had done since antiquity, but even did not want their land or goods to be made over to their communities. By so doing they meant to bear witness to an extremely modest life, to show solidarity to the poor, and to trust in Providence alone, to live by Providence every day, trustingly placing themselves in God's hands. This personal and community style of the Mendicant Orders, together with total adherence to the teaching and authority of the Church, was deeply appreciated by the Pontiffs of the time, such as Innocent III and Honorius III, who gave their full support to the new ecclesial experiences, recognizing in them the voice of the Spirit. And results were not lacking: the groups of paupers that had separated from the Church returned to ecclesial communion or were gradually reduced until they disappeared.

Today too, although we live in a society in which "having" often prevails over "being," we are very sensitive to the examples of poverty and solidarity that believers offer by their courageous decisions. Today too, similar projects are not lacking: the movements, which truly stem from the newness of the Gospel and live it with radicalism in this day and age, placing themselves in God's hands to serve their neighbor. As Paul VI recalled in *Evangelii Nuntiandi,* the world listens willingly to teachers when they are also witnesses. This is a lesson never to be forgotten in the task of spreading the Gospel: to be a mirror reflecting divine love, one must first live what one proclaims.

The Franciscans and Dominicans were not only witnesses but also teachers. In fact, another widespread need in their time was for religious instruction. Many of the lay faithful who dwelled in the rapidly expanding cities wanted to live an intensely spiritual Christian life. They therefore sought to deepen their knowledge of the faith and to be guided in the demanding but exciting path of holiness. The Mendicant Orders were felicitously able to meet this need too: the proclamation of the Gospel in simplicity and with its depth and grandeur was an aim, perhaps the principal aim, of this movement. Indeed, they devoted themselves with great zeal to preaching. Great throngs of the faithful, often true and proper crowds, would gather to listen to the preachers in the churches and in the open air; let us think, for example, of St. Anthony.

The preachers addressed topics close to people's lives, especially the practice of the theological and moral virtues, with practical examples that were easy to understand. They also taught ways to cultivate a life of prayer and devotion. For example, the Franciscans spread far and wide the devotion to the humanity of Christ, with the commitment to imitate the Lord. Thus it is hardly surprising that many of the faithful, men and women, chose to be accompanied on their Christian journey by Franciscan or Dominican Friars, who were much sought after and esteemed spiritual directors and confessors. In this way associations of lay faithful came into being which drew inspiration from the spirituality of St. Francis and St. Dominic as it was adapted to their way of living. In other words, the proposal of a "lay holiness" won many people over. As the Second Ecumenical Vatican Council recalled, the call to holiness is not reserved to the few but is universal (cf. *Lumen Gentium,* n. 40). In all the states of life, in accordance with the demands of each one of them a possibility of living the Gospel may be found. In our day too, each and every Christian must strive for the "high standard of Christian living," whatever the class to which he or she belongs!

The importance of the Mendicant Orders thus grew so vigorously in the Middle Ages that secular institutions, such as the labor organizations, the ancient gilds, and the civil authorities themselves, often had recourse to the spiritual counseling of Members of these Orders in order to draw up their regulations and, at times, to settle both internal and external conflicts. The Franciscans and Dominicans became the spiritual animators of the medieval city. With deep insight they put into practice a pastoral strategy suited to the social changes. Since many people were moving from the countryside to the cities, they no longer built their convents in rural districts but rather in urban zones. Furthermore, to carry out their activities for the benefit of souls, they had to keep abreast of pastoral needs. With another entirely innovative decision, the Mendicant Orders relinquished their principle of stability, a classical principle of ancient monasticism, opting for a different approach. Friars Minor and Preachers travelled with missionary zeal from one place to another. Consequently they organized themselves differently in comparison with the majority of monastic Orders. Instead of the traditional autonomy that every monastery enjoyed, they gave greater importance to the Order as such and to the Superior General, as well as to the struc-

*The Franciscans and Dominicans became the spiritual animators of the medieval city.*

ture of the Provinces. Thus the Mendicants were more available to the needs of the universal Church. Their flexibility enabled them to send out the most suitable friars on specific missions, and the Mendicant Orders reached North Africa, the Middle East, and Northern Europe. With this adaptability, their missionary dynamism was renewed.

The cultural transformations taking place in that period constituted another great challenge. New issues enlivened the discussion in the universities that came into being at the end of the twelfth century. Minors and Preachers did not hesitate to take on this commitment. As students and professors they entered the most famous universities of the time, set up study centers, produced texts of great value, gave life to true and proper schools of thought, were protagonists of scholastic theology in its best period, and had an important effect on the development of thought. The greatest thinkers, St. Thomas Aquinas and St. Bonaventure, were Mendicants who worked precisely with this dynamism of the new evangelization which also renewed the courage of thought, of the dialogue between reason and faith. Today too a "charity of and in the truth" exists, an "intellectual charity" that must be exercised to enlighten minds and to combine faith with culture. The dedication of the Franciscans and Dominicans in the medieval universities is an invitation, dear faithful, to make ourselves present in the places where knowledge is tempered so as to focus the light of the Gospel, with respect and conviction, on the fundamental questions that concern Man, his dignity, and his eternal destiny. Thinking of the role of the Franciscans and the Dominicans in the Middle Ages, of the spiritual renewal they inspired and of the breath of new life they communicated in the world, a monk said: "At that time the world was ageing. Two Orders were born in the Church whose youth they renewed like that of an eagle" (Burchard of Ursperg, *Chronicon*).

Dear brothers and sisters, let us invoke the Holy Spirit, the eternal youth of the Church: may he make each one aware of the urgent need to offer a consistent and courageous Gospel witness so that there may always be saints who make the Church resplendent, like a bride, ever pure and beautiful, without spot or wrinkle, who can attract the world irresistibly to Christ and to his salvation.

# CHAPTER ELEVEN

# St. Francis of Assisi[1]

In the previous chapter, I illustrated the providential role the Orders of Friars Minor and the Order of Preachers, founded by St. Francis of Assisi and St. Dominic de Guzmán respectively, played in the renewal of the Church in their day. Now I would like to present the figure of Francis, an authentic "giant" of holiness, who continues to fascinate a great many people of all age groups and every religion.

"A sun was born into the world." With these words, in the Divine Comedy (*Paradiso*, Canto XI), the great Italian poet Dante Alighieri alludes to Francis's birth, which took place in Assisi either at the end of 1181 or the beginning of 1182. As part of a rich family — his father was a cloth merchant — Francis lived a carefree adolescence and youth, cultivating the chivalrous ideals of the time. At age twenty, he took part in a military campaign and was taken prisoner. He became ill and was freed. After his return to Assisi, a slow process of spiritual conversion began within him, which brought him to gradually abandon the worldly lifestyle that he had adopted thus far. The famous episodes of Francis's meeting with the leper to whom, dismounting from his horse, he gave the kiss of peace and of the message from the Crucifix in the small Church of St. Damian, date back to this period. Three times Christ on the Cross came to life, and told him: "Go,

---

[1] Pope Benedict XVI, General Audience, January 27, 2010.

Francis, and repair my Church in ruins." This simple occurrence of the word of God heard in the Church of St. Damian contains a profound symbolism. At that moment St. Francis was called to repair the small church, but the ruinous state of the building was a symbol of the dramatic and disquieting situation of the Church herself.

At that time the Church had a superficial faith which did not shape or transform life, a scarcely zealous clergy, and a chilling of love. It was an interior destruction of the Church which also brought a decomposition of unity, with the birth of heretical movements. Yet, there at the center of the Church in ruins was the Crucified Lord, and he spoke: he called for renewal, he called Francis to the manual labor of repairing the small Church of St. Damian, the symbol of a much deeper call to renew Christ's own Church, with her radicality of faith and her loving enthusiasm for Christ. This event, which probably happened in 1205, calls to mind another similar occurrence which took place in 1207: Pope Innocent III's dream. In it, he saw the Basilica of St. John Lateran, the mother of all churches, collapsing and one small and insignificant religious brother supporting the church on his shoulders to prevent it from falling. On the one hand, it is interesting to note that it is not the Pope who was helping to prevent the church from collapsing but rather a small and insignificant brother, whom the Pope recognized in Francis when he later came to visit. Innocent III was a powerful Pope who had a great theological formation and great political influence; nevertheless he was not the one to renew the Church but the small, insignificant religious. It was St. Francis, called by God. On the other hand, however, it is important to note that St. Francis does not renew the Church without or in opposition to the Pope, but only in communion with him. The two realities go together: the Successor of Peter, the bishops, the Church founded on the succession of the Apostles and the new charism that the Holy Spirit brought to life at that time for the Church's renewal. Authentic renewal grew from these together.

Let us return to the life of St. Francis. When his father Bernardone reproached him for being too generous to the poor, Francis, standing before the bishop of Assisi, in a symbolic gesture, stripped off his clothes, thus showing he renounced his paternal inheritance. Just as at the moment of creation, Francis had nothing, only the life that God gave him, into whose hands he delivered himself. He then lived as a hermit, until, in 1208, another fundamental step in his journey of conversion took place. While listening to a passage from the Gospel of Matthew, Jesus's discourse to the apostles whom he sent out on mission, Francis felt called to live in poverty and dedicate himself to preaching. Other companions joined him, and in 1209 he travelled to Rome, to propose to Pope Innocent III the plan for a new form of Christian life. He received a fatherly welcome from that great Pontiff, who, enlightened by the Lord, perceived the divine origin of the movement inspired by Francis. The *Poverello* of Assisi understood that every charism as a gift of the Holy Spirit existed to serve the Body of Christ, which is the Church; therefore he always acted in full communion with the ecclesial authorities. In the life of the saints there is no contradiction between prophetic charism and the charism of governance, and if tension arises, they know to patiently await the times determined by the Holy Spirit.

Actually, several nineteenth-century and also twentieth-century historians have sought to construct a so-called historical Francis, behind the traditional depiction of the saint, just as they sought to create a so-called historical Jesus behind the Jesus of the Gospels. This historical Francis would not have been a man of the Church, but rather a man connected directly and solely to Christ, a man who wanted to bring about a renewal of the People of God, without canonical forms or hierarchy. The truth is that St. Francis really did have an extremely intimate relationship with Jesus and with the word of God, that he wanted to pursue *sine glossa*: just as it is, in all its radicality and truth. It is also true that initially he did not intend to create an Order with the necessary canonical forms. Rather he simply wanted, through the word of God and the presence of the Lord, to renew the People of God, to call them back to listening to the word and to literal obedience to Christ. Furthermore, he knew that Christ was never "mine" but is always "ours," that "I" cannot possess Christ, that "I" cannot rebuild in opposition to the Church, her will, and her teaching. Instead it is only in communion with the Church built on the Apostolic succession that obedience, too, to the word of God can be renewed.

It is also true that Francis had no intention of creating a new Order, but solely that of renewing the People of God for the Lord who comes. He understood, however, through suffering and pain that everything must have its own order and that the law of the Church is necessary to give shape to renewal. Thus he placed himself fully, with his heart, in communion with the Church, with the Pope and with the bishops. He always knew that the center of the Church is the Eucharist, where the Body of Christ and his Blood are made present through the priesthood, the Eucharist, and the communion of the Church. Wherever the priesthood and the Eucharist and the Church come together, it is there alone that the word of God also dwells. The real historical Francis was the Francis of the Church, and precisely in this way he continues to speak to nonbelievers and believers of other confessions and religions as well.

Francis and his friars, who were becoming ever more numerous, established themselves at the Portiuncula, or the Church of

Santa Maria degli Angeli, the sacred place par excellence of Franciscan spirituality. Even Clare, a young woman of Assisi from a noble family, followed the school of Francis. This became the origin of the Second Franciscan Order, that of the Poor Clares, another experience destined to produce outstanding figures of sainthood in the Church.

Innocent III's successor, Pope Honorius III, with his Bull *Cum Dilecti* in 1218 supported the unique development of the first Friars Minor, who started missions in different European countries, and even in Morocco. In 1219 Francis obtained permission to visit and speak to the Muslim sultan Malik al-Klmil, to preach the Gospel of Jesus there too. I would like to highlight this episode in St. Francis's life, which is very timely. In an age when there was a conflict underway between Christianity and Islam, Francis, intentionally armed only with his faith and personal humility, travelled the path of dialogue effectively. The chronicles tell us that he was given a benevolent welcome and a cordial reception by the Muslim Sultan. It provides a model which should inspire today's relations between Christians and Muslims: to promote a sincere dialogue, in reciprocal respect and mutual understanding (cf. *Nostra Aetate*, 3). It appears that later, in 1220, Francis visited the Holy Land, thus sowing a seed that would bear much fruit: his spiritual sons would in fact make of the sites where Jesus lived a privileged space for their mission. It is with gratitude that I think today of the great merits of the Franciscan Custody of the Holy Land.

On his return to Italy, Francis turned over the administration of his Order to his vicar, Br. Pietro Cattani, while the Pope

> *In an age when there was a conflict underway between Christianity and Islam, Francis, intentionally armed only with his faith and personal humility, travelled the path of dialogue effectively.*

entrusted the rapidly growing Order's protection to Cardinal Ugolino, the future Supreme Pontiff Gregory IX. For his part, the founder, dedicated completely to his preaching, which he carried out with great success, compiled his Rule that was then approved by the Pope.

In 1224, at the hermitage in La Verna, Francis had a vision of the Crucified Lord in the form of a seraph and from that encounter received the stigmata from the Seraph Crucifix, thus becoming one with the Crucified Christ. It was a gift, therefore, that expressed his intimate identification with the Lord.

The death of Francis, his *transitus*, occurred on the evening of October 3, 1226, in the Portiuncula. After having blessed his spiritual children, he died, lying on the bare earthen floor. Two years later Pope Gregory IX entered him in the roll of saints. A short time after, a great basilica in his honor was constructed in Assisi, still today an extremely popular pilgrim destination. There pilgrims can venerate the saint's tomb and take in the frescoes by Giotto, an artist who has magnificently illustrated Francis's life.

It has been said that Francis represents an *alter Christus*, that he was truly a living icon of Christ. He has also been called "the brother of Jesus." Indeed, this was his ideal: to be like Jesus, to contemplate Christ in the Gospel, to love him intensely and to imitate his virtues. In particular, he wished to ascribe interior and exterior poverty with a fundamental value, which he also taught to his spiritual sons. The first Beatitude of the Sermon on the Mount "Blessed are the poor in spirit, for theirs is the kingdom of heaven" (Matthew 5: 3) found a luminous fulfillment in the life and words of St. Francis. Truly, dear friends, the saints are the best interpreters of the Bible. As they incarnate the word of God in their own lives, they make it more captivating than ever, so that it really speaks to us. The witness of Francis, who loved poverty as a means to follow Christ with dedication and total freedom, continues to be for us too an invitation to cultivate interior poverty in order to grow in our trust of God, also by adopting a sober lifestyle and a detachment from material goods.

Francis's love for Christ expressed itself in a special way in the adoration of the Blessed Sacrament of the Eucharist. In the *Fonti Francescane* (Writings of St. Francis) one reads such moving expressions as: "Let everyone be struck with fear, let the whole world tremble, and let the heavens exult, when Christ, the Son of the living God, is present on the altar in the hands of a priest. Oh stupendous dignity! O humble sublimity, that the Lord of the universe, God and the Son of God, so humbles himself that for our salvation he hides himself under an ordinary piece of bread" (Francis of Assisi, *Scritti*, Editrici Francescane, Padova 2002, 401).

I would like to recall a piece of advice that Francis gave to priests: "When you wish to celebrate Mass, in a pure way, reverently make the true sacrifice of the Most Holy Body and Blood of our Lord Jesus Christ" (Francis of Assisi, *Scritti*, 399). Francis always showed great deference toward priests, and asserted that they should always be treated with respect, even in cases where they might be somewhat unworthy personally. The reason he gave for this profound respect was that they receive the gift of consecrating the Eucharist. Dear brothers in the priesthood, let us never forget this teaching: the holiness of the Eucharist appeals to us to be pure, to live in a way that is consistent with the Mystery we celebrate.

From love for Christ stems love for others and also for all God's creatures. This is yet another characteristic trait of Francis's spirituality: the sense of universal brotherhood and love for Creation, which inspired the famous *Canticle of Creatures*. This too is an extremely timely message. As I recalled in my Encyclical *Caritas in Veritate*, development is sustainable only when it respects Creation and does not damage the environment (cf. nn. 48–52), and in my Message for the World Day of Peace for 2010, I also underscored that even building stable peace is linked to respect for Creation. Francis reminds us that the wisdom and benevolence of the Creator is expressed through Creation. He understood nature as a language in which God speaks to us, in which reality becomes clear, and we can speak *of* God and *with* God.

Dear friends, Francis was a great saint and a joyful man. His simplicity, his humility, his faith, his love for Christ, his goodness toward every man and every woman, brought him gladness in every circumstance. Indeed, there subsists an intimate and indissoluble relationship between holiness and joy. A French writer once wrote that there is only one sorrow in the world: not to be saints, that is, not to be near to God. Looking at the testimony of St. Francis, we understand that this is the secret of true happiness: to become saints, close to God!

May the Virgin, so tenderly loved by Francis, obtain this gift for us. Let us entrust ourselves to her with the words of the *Poverello* of Assisi himself: "Blessed Virgin Mary, no one like you among women has ever been born in the world, daughter and handmaid of the Most High King and heavenly Father, Mother of our Most Blessed Lord Jesus Christ, spouse of the Holy Spirit. Pray for us ... to your most blessed and beloved Son, Lord and Master" (Francesco di Assisi, *Scritti*, 163).

# CHAPTER TWELVE

# St. Dominic Guzmán[1]

In the last chapter I presented the luminous figure of Francis of Assisi. Now I want to reflect on another saint of the same period who made a fundamental contribution to the renewal of the Church of his time: St. Dominic, the Founder of the Order of Preachers, also known as Dominican Friars.

His successor at the head of the Order, Bl. Jordan of Saxony, gives a complete picture of St. Dominic in the text of a famous prayer: "Your strong love burned with heavenly fire and God-like zeal. With all the fervor of an impetuous heart and with an avowal of perfect poverty, you spent your whole self in the cause of the Apostolic life" and in preaching the Gospel. It is precisely this fundamental trait of Dominic's witness that is emphasized: he always spoke *with* God and *of* God. Love for the Lord and for neighbor, the search for God's glory and the salvation of souls in the lives of saints always go hand in hand.

Dominic was born at Caleruega, Spain, in about 1170. He belonged to a noble family of Old Castile and, supported by a priest uncle, was educated at a famous school in Palencia. He distinguished himself straight away for his interest in the study of Sacred Scripture and for his love of the poor, to the point of selling books, that in his time were a very valuable asset, in order to support famine victims with the proceeds.

---

[1] Pope Benedict XVI, General Audience, February 3, 2010.

Ordained a priest, he was elected canon of the Cathedral Chapter in Osma, his native diocese. Although he may well have thought that this appointment might bring him a certain amount of prestige in the Church and in society, he did not view it as a personal privilege or as the beginning of a brilliant ecclesiastical career but, rather, as a service to carry out with dedication and humility. Are not a career and power temptations from which not even those who have a role of guidance and governance in the Church are exempt? I recalled this during the consecration of several bishops on September 16, 2009: "We do not seek power, prestige or esteem for ourselves.... We know how in civil society and often also in the Church things suffer because many people on whom responsibility has been conferred work for themselves rather than for the community."

The Bishop of Osma, a true and zealous Pastor whose name was Didacus, soon spotted Dominic's spiritual qualities and wanted to avail himself of his collaboration. Together they went to Northern Europe, on the diplomatic missions entrusted to them by the King of Castile. On his travels Dominic became aware of two enormous challenges for the Church of his time: the existence of people who were not yet evangelized on the northern boundaries of the European continent, and the religious schism that undermined Christian life in the South of France where the activity of certain heretical groups was creating a disturbance and distancing people from the truth of the faith. So it was that missionary action for those who did not know the light of the Gospel and the work of the re-evangelization of Christian communities became the apostolic goals that Dominic resolved to pursue.

It was the Pope, to whom the Bishop Didacus and Dominic went to seek advice, who asked Dominic to devote himself to preaching to the Albigensians, a heretical group which upheld a dualistic conception of reality, that is, with two equally powerful creator principles, Good and Evil. This group consequently despised matter as coming from the principle of evil. They even refused marriage, and went to the point of denying the Incarnation of Christ and the sacraments in which the Lord "touches" us through matter, and the resurrection of bodies. The Albigensians esteemed the poor and austere life — in this regard they were even exemplary — and criticized the riches of the clergy of that time. Dominic enthusiastically accepted this mission and carried it out with the example of his own poor and austere existence, Gospel preaching, and public discussions. He devoted the rest of his life to this mission of preaching the Good News. His sons were also to make St. Dominic's other dreams come true: the mission *ad gentes,* that is, to those who do not yet know Jesus and the mission to those who lived in the cities, especially the university cities where the new intellectual trends were a challenge to the faith of the cultured.

This great saint reminds us that in the heart of the Church a missionary fire must always burn. It must be a constant incentive to make the first proclamation of the Gospel and, wherever necessary, a new evangelization. Christ, in fact, is the most precious good that the men and women of every time and every place have the right to know and love! And it is comforting to see that in the Church today too there are many pastors and lay faithful alike, members of ancient religious orders and new ecclesial movements who spend their lives joyfully for this supreme ideal, proclaiming and witnessing to the Gospel!

Many other men then joined Dominic de Guzmán, attracted by the same aspiration. In this manner, after the first foundation in Toulouse, the Order of Preachers gradually came into being. Dominic in fact, in perfect obedience to the directives of the Popes of his time — Innocent III and Honorius III — used the ancient Rule of St. Augustine, adapting it to the needs of apostolic life that led him and his companions to preach as they travelled from one place to another but then returning to their own convents and places of study, to prayer and community life. Dominic wanted to give special importance to two values he deemed indispensable for the success of the evangelizing mission: community life in poverty and study.

First of all Dominic and the Friars Preachers presented themselves as mendicants, that is, without vast estates to be administered. This element made them more available for study and itinerant preaching and constituted a practical witness for the people. The internal government of the Dominican convents and provinces was structured on the system of chapters which elected their own superiors, who were subsequently confirmed by the major superiors; thus it was an organization that stimulated fraternal life and the responsibility of all the members of the community, demanding strong personal convictions. The choice of this system was born precisely from the fact that as preachers of the truth of God, the Dominicans had to be consistent with what they proclaimed. The truth studied and shared in charity with the brethren is the deepest foundation of joy. Bl. Jordan of Saxony said of St. Dominic: "All men were swept into the embrace of his charity, and, in loving all, he was beloved by all.... He claimed it his right to rejoice with the joyful and to weep with the sorrowful" (*Libellus de principiis Ordinis Praedicatorum autore Iordano de Saxonia*, ed. H.C. Scheeben [*Monumenta Historica Sancti Patris Nostri Dominici*, Romae, 1935].

Secondly, with a courageous gesture, Dominic wanted his followers to acquire a sound theological training and did not hesitate to send them to the universities of the time, even though

*The truth studied and shared in charity with the brethren is the deepest foundation of joy.*

a fair number of clerics viewed these cultural institutions with diffidence. The Constitutions of the Order of Preachers give great importance to study as a preparation for the apostolate. Dominic wanted his Friars to devote themselves to it without reserve, with diligence and with piety; a study based on the soul of all theological knowledge, that is, on Sacred Scripture, and respectful of the questions asked by reason. The development of culture requires those who carry out the ministry of the Word at various levels to be well trained. I therefore urge all those, pastors and lay people alike, to cultivate this "cultural dimension" of faith, so that the beauty of the Christian truth may be better understood and faith may be truly nourished, reinforced, and also defended. I ask seminarians and priests to esteem the spiritual value of study. The quality of the priestly ministry also depends on the generosity with which one applies oneself to the study of the revealed truths.

Dominic, who wished to found a religious Order of theologian-preachers, reminds us that theology has a spiritual and pastoral dimension that enriches the soul and life. Priests, the consecrated, and also all the faithful may find profound "inner joy" in contemplating the beauty of the truth that comes from God, a truth that is ever timely and ever alive. Moreover the motto of the Friars Preachers *contemplata aliis tradere* helps us to discover a pastoral yearning in the contemplative study of this truth because of the need to communicate to others the fruit of one's own contemplation.

When Dominic died in 1221 in Bologna, the city that declared him its Patron, his work had already had widespread success. The Order of Preachers, with the Holy See's support, had spread to many countries in Europe for the benefit of the whole Church. Dominic was canonized in 1234, and it is he himself who, with his holiness, points out to us two indispensable means for making apostolic action effective. In the very first place is Marian devotion which he fostered tenderly and left as a precious legacy to his spiritual sons who, in the history of the Church, have had the great merit of disseminating the prayer of the Holy Rosary, so dear to the Christian people and so rich in Gospel values: a true school of faith and piety. In the second place, Dominic, who cared for several women's monasteries in France and in Rome, believed unquestioningly in the value of prayers of intercession for the success of the apostolic work. Only in heaven will we understand how much the prayer of cloistered religious effectively accompanies apostolic action! To each and every one of them I address my grateful and affectionate thoughts.

Dear brothers and sisters, may the life of Dominic de Guzmán spur us all to be fervent in prayer, courageous in living out our faith and deeply in love with Jesus Christ. Through his intercession, let us ask God always to enrich the Church with authentic preachers of the Gospel.

# CHAPTER THIRTEEN

# St. Anthony of Padua[1]

I presented St. Francis of Assisi in a previous chapter. Now I would like to introduce another saint who belonged to the first generation of the Friars Minor: Anthony of Padua, or of Lisbon, as he is also called with reference to his native town. He is one of the most popular saints in the whole Catholic Church, venerated not only in Padua, where a splendid Basilica has been built that contains his mortal remains, but also throughout the world. Dear to the faithful are the images and statues that portray him with the lily a symbol of his purity or with the Child Jesus in his arms, in memory of a miraculous apparition mentioned in several literary sources.

With his outstanding gifts of intelligence, balance, apostolic zeal and, primarily, mystic fervor, Anthony contributed significantly to the development of Franciscan spirituality.

He was born into a noble family in Lisbon in about 1195 and was baptized with the name of Fernando. He entered the Canons who followed the monastic Rule of St. Augustine, first at St. Vincent's Monastery in Lisbon and later at that of the Holy Cross in Coimbra, a renowned cultural center in Portugal. He dedicated himself with interest and solicitude to the study of the Bible and of the Church Fathers, acquiring the theological knowledge that was to bear fruit in his teaching and preaching

---

[1] Pope Benedict XVI, General Audience, February 10, 2010.

activities. The event that represented a decisive turning point in his life happened in Coimbra. It was there, in 1220, that the relics were exposed of the first five Franciscan missionaries who had gone to Morocco, where they had met with martyrdom. Their story inspired in young Fernando the desire to imitate them and to advance on the path of Christian perfection. Thus he asked to leave the Augustinian Canons to become a Friar Minor. His request was granted and, having taken the name of Anthony, he too set out for Morocco, but divine Providence disposed otherwise.

After an illness he was obliged to return to Italy and, in 1221, participated in the famous "Chapter of the Mats" in Assisi, where he also met St. Francis. He then lived for a period in complete concealment in a convent at Forlì in northern Italy, where the Lord called him to another mission. Invited, in somewhat casual circumstances, to preach on the occasion of a priestly ordination, he showed himself to be endowed with such knowledge and eloquence that the Superiors assigned him to preaching. Thus he embarked on apostolic work in Italy and France that was so intense and effective that it induced many people who had left the Church to retrace their footsteps. Anthony was also one of the first if not the first theology teachers of the Friars Minor. He began his teaching in Bologna with the blessing of St. Francis who, recognizing Anthony's virtues, sent him a short letter that began with these words: "I would like you to teach the brethren theology." Anthony laid the foundations of Franciscan theology which, cultivated by other outstanding thinkers, was to reach its apex with St. Bonaventure of Bagnoregio and Bl. Duns Scotus.

Having become Provincial Superior of the Friars Minor in northern Italy, he continued his ministry of preaching, alternating it with his office of governance. When his term as Provincial came to an end, he withdrew to a place near Padua where he had stayed on various other occasions. Barely a year later, he died at the city gates on June 13, 1231. Padua, which had welcomed him with affection and veneration in his lifetime, has always accorded him honor and devotion. Pope Gregory IX himself, having heard him preach, described him as the "Ark of the Testament" and subsequent to miracles brought about through his intercession canonized him in 1232, only a year after his death.

In the last period of his life, Anthony put in writing two cycles of "Sermons," entitled respectively "Sunday Sermons" and "Sermons on the Saints" destined for the Franciscan Order's preachers and teachers of theological studies. In these Sermons he commented on the texts of Scripture presented by the Liturgy, using the patristic and medieval interpretation of the four senses: the literal or historical, the allegorical or Christological, the tropological or moral, and the anagogical, which orients a person to eternal life. Today it has been rediscovered that these senses are dimensions of the one meaning of Sacred Scripture and that it is right to interpret Sacred Scripture by seeking the four dimensions of its words. St. Anthony's sermons are theological and homiletical texts that echo the live preaching in which Anthony proposes a true and proper itinerary of Christian life. The richness of spiritual teaching contained in the "Sermons" was so great that in 1946 Ven. Pope Pius XII proclaimed Anthony a Doctor of the Church, attributing to him the title "Doctor Evangelicus," since the freshness and beauty of the Gospel emerge from these writings. We can still read them today with great spiritual profit.

In these Sermons St. Anthony speaks of prayer as of a loving relationship that impels man to speak gently with the Lord, creating an ineffable joy that sweetly enfolds the soul in prayer. Anthony reminds us that prayer requires an atmosphere of silence, which does not mean distance from external noise but rather is an interior experience that aims to remove the distractions caused by a soul's anxieties, thereby creating silence in the soul itself. According to this prominent Franciscan Doctor's teaching, prayer is structured in four indispensable attitudes which in Anthony's Latin are defined as *obsecratio, oratio, postulatio, gratiarum actio.* We might translate them in the following manner. The first step in prayer is confidently opening one's heart to God; this is not merely accepting a word but opening one's heart to God's presence. Next, is speaking with him affectionately, seeing him present with oneself; then a very natural thing presenting our needs to him; and lastly, praising and thanking him.

In St. Anthony's teaching on prayer we perceive one of the specific traits of the Franciscan theology that he founded: namely the role assigned to divine love which enters into the sphere of the affections, of the will and of the heart, and which is also the source from which flows a spiritual knowledge that surpasses all other knowledge. In fact, it is in loving that we come to know.

Anthony writes further: "Charity is the soul of faith, it gives it life; without love, faith dies" (*Sermones Dominicales et Festivi* II, Messagero, Padua 1979, p. 37).

It is only the prayerful soul that can progress in spiritual life: this is the privileged object of St. Anthony's preaching. He is thoroughly familiar with the shortcomings of human nature, with our tendency to lapse into sin, which is why he continuously urges us to fight the inclination to avidity, pride, and impurity; instead of practicing the virtues of poverty and generosity, of humility and obedience, of chastity and of purity. At the beginning of the thirteenth century, in the context of the rebirth of the city and the flourishing of trade, the number of people who were insensitive to the needs of the poor increased. This is why on various occasions Anthony invites the faithful to think of the true riches, those of the heart, which make people good and merciful and permit them to lay up treasure in Heaven. "O rich people," he urged them, "befriend ... the poor, welcome them into your homes: it will subsequently be they who receive you in the eternal tabernacles in which is the beauty of peace, the confidence of security and the opulent tranquility of eternal satiety" (*ibid.,* p. 29).

Is not this, dear friends, perhaps a very important teaching today too, when the financial crisis and serious economic inequalities impoverish many people and create conditions of poverty? In my Encyclical *Caritas in Veritate* I recall: "The economy needs ethics in order to function correctly, not any ethics whatsoever, but an ethics which is people-centered" (n. 45).

Anthony, in the school of Francis, always put Christ at the center of his life and thinking, of his action, and of his preaching. This is another characteristic feature of Franciscan theology: Christocentrism. Franciscan theology willingly contemplates and invites others to contemplate the mysteries of the Lord's humanity, the man Jesus, and in a special way the mystery of the Nativity: God who made himself a Child and gave himself into our hands, a mystery that gives rise to sentiments of love and gratitude for divine goodness.

Not only the Nativity, a central point of Christ's love for humanity, but also the vision of the Crucified One inspired in Anthony thoughts of gratitude to God and esteem for the dignity of the human person, so that all believers and nonbelievers might find in the Crucified One and in his image a life-enriching meaning. St. Anthony writes: "Christ who is your life is hanging before you, so that you may look at the Cross as in a mirror. There you will be able to know how mortal were your wounds, that no medicine other than the Blood of the Son of God could heal. If you look closely, you will be able to realize how great your human dignity and your value are.... Nowhere other than looking at himself in the mirror of the Cross can man better understand how much he is worth" (*Sermones Dominicales et Festivi* III, pp. 213–214).

In meditating on these words we are better able to understand the importance of the image of the Crucified One for our culture, for our humanity that is born from the Christian faith. Precisely by looking at the Crucified One we see, as St. Anthony says, how great are the dignity and worth of the human being. At no other point can we understand how much the human person is worth, precisely because God makes us so important, considers us so important that, in his opinion, we are worthy of his suffering; thus all human dignity appears in the mirror of the Crucified One and our gazing upon him is ever a source of acknowledgment of human dignity.

Dear friends, may Anthony of Padua, so widely venerated by the faithful, intercede for the whole Church and especially for those who are dedicated to preaching; let us pray the Lord that he will help us learn a little of this art from St. Anthony. May preachers, drawing inspiration from his example, be effective in their communication by taking pains to combine solid and sound doctrine with sincere and fervent devotion. Let us pray that priests and deacons will carry out with concern this ministry of the proclamation of the word of God, making it timely for the faithful, especially through liturgical homilies. May they effectively present the eternal beauty of Christ, just as Anthony recommended: "If you preach Jesus, he will melt hardened hearts; if you invoke him he will soften harsh temptations; if you think of him he will enlighten your mind; if you read of him he will satisfy your intellect" (*Sermones Dominicales et Festivi* III, p. 59).

# CHAPTER FOURTEEN

# St. Bonaventure

## HIS LIFE[1]

I confide that in broaching the subject of St. Bonaventure of Bagnoregio I feel a certain nostalgia, for I am thinking back to my research as a young scholar on this author who was particularly dear to me. My knowledge of him had quite an impact on my formation. In September of 2009, with great joy, I made a pilgrimage to the place of his birth, Bagnoregio, an Italian town in Lazio that venerates his memory.

St. Bonaventure, in all likelihood born in 1217, died in 1274. Thus he lived in the thirteenth century, an epoch in which the Christian faith which had deeply penetrated the culture and society of Europe inspired imperishable works in the fields of literature, the visual arts, philosophy, and theology. Among the great Christian figures who contributed to the composition of this harmony between faith and culture Bonaventure stands out, a man of action and contemplation, of profound piety and prudent government.

He was called Giovanni di Fidanza. An episode that occurred when he was still a boy deeply marked his life, as he himself recounts. He fell seriously ill, and even his father, who was a doctor, gave up all hope of saving him from death. So his mother had recourse to the intercession of St. Francis of Assisi, who had recently been canonized. And Giovanni recovered.

---

[1] Pope Benedict XVI, General Audience, March 3, 2010.

The figure of the *Poverello* of Assisi became even more familiar to him several years later when he was in Paris, where he had gone to pursue his studies. He had obtained a Master of Arts Diploma, which we could compare with that of a prestigious secondary school in our time. At that point, like so many young men in the past and also today, Giovanni asked himself a crucial question: "What should I do with my life?" Fascinated by the witness of fervor and evangelical radicalism of the Friars Minor who had arrived in Paris in 1219, Giovanni knocked at the door of the Franciscan convent in that city and asked to be admitted to the great family of St. Francis's disciples. Many years later he explained the reasons for his decision: he recognized Christ's action in St. Francis and in the movement he had founded. Thus he wrote in a letter addressed to another friar: "I confess before God that the reason which made me love the life of blessed Francis most is that it resembled the birth and early development of the Church. The Church began with simple fishermen, and was subsequently enriched by very distinguished and wise teachers; the religion of Blessed Francis was not established by the prudence of men but by Christ" (*Epistula de tribus quaestionibus ad magistrum innominatum,* in *Opere di San Bonaventura. Introduzione generale,* Rome 1990, p. 29).

So it was that in about the year 1243 Giovanni was clothed in the Franciscan habit and took the name "Bonaventure." He was immediately sent to study and attended the Faculty of Theology of the University of Paris where he took a series of very demanding courses. He obtained the various qualifications required for an academic career earning a bachelor's degree in Scripture and in the *Sentences.* Thus Bonaventure studied profoundly Sacred Scripture, the *Sentences* of Peter Lombard — the theology manual in that time — and the most important theological authors. He was in contact with the teachers and students from across Europe who converged in Paris, and he developed his own personal thinking and a spiritual sensitivity of great value with which, in the following years, he was able to infuse his works and his sermons, thus becoming one of the most important theologians in the history of the Church. It is important to remember the title of the thesis he defended in order to qualify to teach theology, the *licentia ubique docendi,* as it was then called. His dissertation was entitled *Questions on the knowledge of Christ.* This subject reveals the central role that Christ always played in Bonaventure's life and teaching. We may certainly say that the whole of his thinking was profoundly Christocentric.

*His dissertation was entitled* Questions on the knowledge of Christ. *This subject reveals the central role that Christ always played in Bonaventure's life and teaching.*

In those years in Paris, Bonaventure's adopted city, a violent dispute was raging against the Friars Minor of St. Francis Assisi and the Friars Preachers of St. Dominic de Guzmán. Their right to teach at the university was contested, and doubt was even being cast upon the authenticity of their consecrated life. Of course, the changes introduced by the Mendicant Orders in the way of understanding religious life, of which I have spoken in previous Catecheses, were so entirely new that not everyone managed to understand them. Then it should be added, just as sometimes happens even among sincerely religious people, that human weakness, such as envy and jealousy, came into play. Although Bonaventure was confronted by the opposition of the other university masters, he had already begun to teach at the Franciscans' Chair of theology and, to respond to those who were challenging the Mendicant Orders, he composed a text entitled *Evangelical Perfection.* In this work he shows how the Mendicant Orders, especially the Friars Minor, in practicing the vows of poverty, chastity, and obedience, were following the recommendations of the Gospel itself. Over and above these historical circumstances the teaching that Bonaventure provides in this work of his and in his life remains every timely: the Church is made more luminous and beautiful by the fidelity to their vocation of those sons and daughters of hers who not only put the evangelical precepts into practice but, by the grace of God, are called to observe their counsels and thereby, with their poor, chaste, and obedient way of life, to witness to the Gospel as a source of joy and perfection.

The storm blew over, at least for a while, and through the personal intervention of Pope Alexander VI in 1257, Bonaventure was officially recognized as a doctor and master of the University of Paris. However, he was obliged to relinquish this prestigious office because in that same year the General Chapter of the Order elected him Minister General.

He fulfilled this office for seventeen years with wisdom and dedication, visiting the provinces, writing to his brethren, and at times intervening with some severity to eliminate abuses. When Bonaventure began this service, the Order of Friars Minor had experienced an extraordinary expansion: there were more than 30,000 Friars scattered throughout the West with missionaries in North Africa, the Middle East, and even in Peking. It was necessary to consolidate this expansion and especially, to give it unity of action and of spirit in full fidelity to Francis's charism. In fact different ways of interpreting the message of the Saint of Assisi arose among his followers, and they ran a real risk of an internal split. To avoid this danger, in 1260 the General Chapter of the Order in Narbonne accepted and ratified a text proposed by Bonaventure in which the norms regulating the daily life of the Friars Minor were collected and unified. Bonaventure, however, foresaw that regardless of the wisdom and moderation which inspired the legislative measures, they would not suffice to guarantee communion of spirit and hearts. It was necessary to share the same ideals and the same motivations.

For this reason Bonaventure wished to present the authentic charism of Francis, his life, and his teaching. Thus he zealously collected documents concerning the *Poverello* and listened attentively to the memories of those who had actually known Francis. This inspired a historically well-founded biography of the Saint of Assisi, entitled *Legenda Maior*. It was redrafted more concisely, hence entitled *Legenda minor*. Unlike the Italian term the Latin word does not mean a product of the imagination but, on the contrary, "*Legenda*" means an authoritative text, "to be read" officially. Indeed, the General Chapter of the Friars Minor in 1263, meeting in Pisa, recognized St. Bonaventure's biography as the most faithful portrait of their founder, and so it became the saint's official biography.

What image of St. Francis emerged from the heart and pen of his follower and successor, St. Bonaventure? The key point: Francis is an *alter Christus,* a man who sought Christ passionately. In the love that impelled Francis to imitate Christ, he was entirely conformed to Christ. Bonaventure pointed out this living ideal to all Francis's followers. This ideal, valid for every Christian, yesterday, today, and forever, was also proposed as a program for the Church in the Third Millennium by my Predecessor, Ven. John Paul II. This program, he wrote in his Letter *Novo Millennio Ineunte,* is centered "in Christ himself, who is to be known, loved and imitated, so that in him we may live the life of the Trinity, and with him transform history until its fulfillment in the heavenly Jerusalem" (n. 29).

In 1273, St. Bonaventure experienced another great change in his life. Pope Gregory X wanted to consecrate him a bishop and to appoint him a cardinal. The Pope also asked him to prepare the

Second Ecumenical Council of Lyons, a most important ecclesial event, for the purpose of re-establishing communion between the Latin Church and the Greek Church. Bonaventure dedicated himself diligently to this task but was unable to see the conclusion of this ecumenical session because he died before it ended. An anonymous papal notary composed a eulogy to Bonaventure which gives us a conclusive portrait of this great saint and excellent theologian. "A good, affable, devout and compassionate man, full of virtue, beloved of God and human beings alike.... God in fact had bestowed upon him such grace that all who saw him were pervaded by a love that their hearts could not conceal" (cf. J.G. Bougerol, *Bonaventura*, in A. Vauchez (edited by), *Storia dei santi e della santità cristiana*. Vol. VI. *L'epoca del rinnovamento evangelico*, Milan 191, p. 91).

Let us gather the heritage of this holy Doctor of the Church who reminds us of the meaning of our life with the following words: "On earth ... we may contemplate the divine immensity through reasoning and admiration; in the heavenly homeland, on the other hand, through the vision, when we are likened to God and through ecstasy ... we shall enter into the joy of God" (*La conoscenza di Cristo, q. 6, conclusione,* in *Opere di San Bonaventura. Opuscoli Teologici / 1*, Rome 1993, p. 187).

## HIS WRITINGS [2]

I would like to continue my presentation of St. Bonaventure of Bagnoregio, reflecting on part of his literary opus and on his doctrine.

As I have already said, among St. Bonaventure's various merits was the ability to interpret authentically and faithfully St. Francis of Assisi, whom he venerated and studied with deep

---

[2] Pope Benedict XVI, General Audience, March 10, 2010.

love. In a special way, in St. Bonaventure's day a trend among the Friars Minor known as the "Spirituals" held that St. Francis had ushered in a totally new phase in history and that the "eternal Gospel," of which Revelation speaks, had come to replace the New Testament. This group declared that the Church had now fulfilled her role in history. They said that she had been replaced by a charismatic community of free men guided from within by the Spirit, namely the "Spiritual Franciscans." This group's ideas were based

*He considered the Old Testament as the age of the Father, followed by the time of the Son, the time of the Church.*

on the writings of a Cistercian Abbot, Joachim of Fiore, who died in 1202. In his works he affirmed a Trinitarian rhythm in history. He considered the Old Testament as the age of the Father, followed by the time of the Son, the time of the Church. The third age was to be awaited, that of the Holy Spirit. The whole of history was thus interpreted as a history of progress: from the severity of the Old Testament to the relative freedom of the time of the Son, in the Church, to the full freedom of the Sons of God in the period of the Holy Spirit. This, finally, was also to be the period of peace among mankind, of the reconciliation of peoples and of religions. Joachim of Fiore had awakened the hope that the new age would stem from a new form of monasticism. Thus it is understandable that a group of Franciscans might have thought it recognized St. Francis of Assisi as the initiator of the new epoch and his Order as the community of the new period, the community of the Age of the Holy Spirit that left behind the hierarchical Church in order to begin the new Church of the Spirit, no longer linked to the old structures.

Hence they ran the risk of very seriously misunderstanding St. Francis's message, of his humble fidelity to the Gospel and to the Church. This error entailed an erroneous vision of Christianity as a whole.

St. Bonaventure, who became Minister General of the Franciscan Order in 1257, had to confront grave tension in his Order precisely because of those who supported the above-mentioned trend of the "Franciscan Spirituals" who followed Joachim of Fiore. To respond to this group and to restore unity to the Order, St. Bonaventure painstakingly studied the authentic writings of Joachim of Fiore, as well as those attributed to him and, bearing in mind the need to present the figure and message of his beloved St. Francis correctly, he wanted to set down a correct view of the theology of history. St. Bonaventure actually tackled the problem in his last work, a collection of conferences for the monks of the studium in Paris. He did not complete it, and it has come down to us through the transcriptions of those who heard him. It is entitled *Hexaëmeron,* in other words an allegorical explanation of the six days of the Creation. The Fathers of the Church considered the six or seven days of the Creation narrative as a prophecy of the history of the world, of humanity. For them, the seven days represented seven periods of history, later also interpreted as seven millennia. With Christ we should have entered the last, that is, the sixth period of history that was to be followed by the great sabbath of God. St. Bonaventure hypothesizes this historical interpretation of the account of the days of the Creation, but in a very free and innovative way. To his mind two phenomena of his time required a new interpretation of the course of history.

The first: the figure of St. Francis, the man totally united with Christ even to communion with the stigmata, almost an *alter Christus,* and, with St. Francis, the new community he created, different from the monasticism known until then. This phenomenon called for a new interpretation, as an innovation of God which appeared at that moment.

The second: the position of Joachim of Fiore who announced a new monasticism and a totally new period of history, going beyond the revelation of the New Testament, demanded a response. As Minister General of the Franciscan Order, St. Bonaventure had immediately realized that with the spiritualistic conception inspired by Joachim of Fiore, the Order would become ungovernable and logically move toward anarchy. In his opinion this had two consequences:

> The first, the practical need for structures and for insertion into the reality of the hierarchical Church, of the real Church, required a theological foundation. This was partly because the others, those who followed the spiritualist concept, upheld what seemed to have a theological foundation.
>
> The second, while taking into account the necessary realism, made it essential not to lose the newness of the figure of St. Francis.

How did St. Bonaventure respond to the practical and theoretical needs? Here I can only provide a very basic summary of his answer, and it is in certain aspects incomplete:

1. St. Bonaventure rejected the idea of the Trinitarian rhythm of history. God is one for all history and is not tritheistic. Hence history is one, even if it is a journey and, according to St. Bonaventure, a journey of progress.

2. Jesus Christ is God's last word — in him God said all, giving and expressing himself. More than himself, God cannot express or give. The Holy Spirit is the Spirit of the Father and of the Son. Christ himself says of the Holy Spirit: "He will bring to your remembrance all that I have said to you" (Jn 14: 26), and "he will take what is mine and declare it to you" (Jn 16: 15). Thus there is no loftier Gospel, there is no other Church to await.

Therefore the Order of St. Francis too must fit into this Church, into her faith, and into her hierarchical order.

3. This does not mean that the Church is stationary, fixed in the past, or that there can be no newness within her. *"Opera Christi non deficiunt, sed proficient"*: Christ's works do not go backwards, they do not fail but progress, the saint said in his letter *De Tribus Quaestionibus*. Thus St. Bonaventure explicitly formulates the idea of progress, and this is an innovation in comparison with the Fathers of the Church and the majority of his contemporaries. For St. Bonaventure Christ was no longer the end of history, as he was for the Fathers of the Church, but rather its center; history does not end with Christ but begins a new period. The following is another consequence: until that moment the idea that the Fathers of the Church were the absolute summit of theology predominated, all successive generations could only be their disciples. St. Bonaventure also recognized the Fathers as teachers forever, but the phenomenon of St. Francis assured him that the riches of Christ's word are inexhaustible and that new light could also appear to the new generations. The oneness of Christ also guarantees newness and renewal in all the periods of history.

The Franciscan Order of course, as he emphasized, belongs to the Church of Jesus Christ, to the apostolic Church, and cannot be built on utopian spiritualism. Yet, at the same time, the newness of this Order in comparison with classical monasticism was valid, and St. Bonaventure, as I said in my previous Catechesis, defended this newness against the attacks of the secular clergy of Paris: the Franciscans have no fixed monastery, they may go everywhere to proclaim the Gospel. It was precisely the break with stability, the characteristic of monasticism, for the sake of a new flexibility that restored to the Church her missionary dynamism.

At this point it might be useful to say that today too there are views that see the entire history of the Church in the second millennium as a gradual decline. Some see this decline as having already begun immediately after the New Testament. In fact, *"Opera Christi non deficiunt, sed proficient"*: Christ's works do not go backwards but forwards. What would the Church be without the new spirituality of the Cistercians, the Franciscans, and the Dominicans, the spirituality of St. Teresa of Ávila and St. John of the Cross and so forth? This affirmation applies today too: *"Opera Christi non deficiunt, sed proficient,"* they move forward. St. Bonaventure teaches us the need for overall, even strict discernment, sober realism, and openness to the newness which Christ gives his Church through the Holy Spirit. And while this idea of decline is repeated, another idea, this "spiritualistic utopianism" is also reiterated. Indeed, we know that after the Second Vatican Council some were convinced that everything was new, that there was a different Church, that the pre-Conciliar Church was finished and that we had another, totally "other" Church, an anarchic utopianism! And thanks be to God the wise helmsmen of the Barque of St. Peter, Pope Paul VI and Pope John Paul II, on the one hand defended the newness of the Council, and on the other, defended the oneness and continuity of the Church, which is always a Church of sinners and always a place of grace.

4. In this regard, St. Bonaventure, as Minister General of the Franciscans, took a line of government which showed clearly that the new Order could not, as a community, live at the same "eschatological height" as St. Francis, in whom he saw the future world anticipated, but guided at the same time by healthy realism and by spiritual courage, he had to come as close as possible to the maximum realization of the Sermon on the Mount, which for St. Francis was *the* rule, but nevertheless bearing in mind the limitations of the human being who is marked by original sin.

Thus we see that for St. Bonaventure governing was not merely action but above all was thinking and praying. At the root of his government we always find prayer and thought; all his decisions are the result of reflection, of thought illumined by prayer. His intimate contact with Christ always accompanied his work as Minister General and therefore he composed a series of theological and mystical writings that express the soul of his government. They also manifest his intention of guiding the Order inwardly, that is, of governing not only by means of commands and structures, but by guiding and illuminating souls, orienting them to Christ.

I would like to mention only one of these writings, which are the soul of his government and point out the way to follow, both for the individual and for the community: the *Itinerarium mentis in Deum* [*The Mind's Road to God*], which is a "manual" for mystical contemplation. This book was conceived in a deeply spiritual place: Mount La Verna, where St. Francis had received the stigmata. In the introduction the author describes the circumstances that gave rise to this writing: "While I meditated on the possible ascent of the mind to God, amongst other things there occurred that miracle which happened in the same place to the blessed Francis himself, namely the vision of the winged Seraph in the form of a Crucifix. While meditating upon this vision, I immediately saw that it offered me the ecstatic contemplation of Fr. Francis himself as well as the way that leads to it" (cf. *The Mind's Road to God,* Prologue, 2, in *Opere di San Bonaventura. Opuscoli Teologici* / 1, Rome 1993, p. 499).

The six wings of the Seraph thus became the symbol of the six stages that lead man progressively from the knowledge of God, through the observation of the world and creatures and through the exploration of the soul itself with its faculties, to the satisfying union with the Trinity through Christ, in imitation of St. Francis of Assisi. The last words of St. Bonaventure's *Itinerarium,* which respond to the question of how it is possible to reach this mystical communion with God, should be made to sink to the depths of the heart: "If you should wish to know how these things come about, (the mystical communion with God) question grace, not instruction; desire, not intellect; the cry of prayer, not pursuit of study; the spouse, not the teacher; God, not man; darkness, not clarity; not light, but the fire that inflames all and transports to God with fullest unction and burning affection.... Let us then ... pass over into darkness; let us impose silence on cares, concupiscence, and phantasms; let us pass over *with the Crucified Christ from this world to the Father,* so that when the Father is shown to us we may say with Philip, *'It is enough for me'"* (cf. *ibid.,* VII 6).

Dear friends, let us accept the invitation addressed to us by St. Bonaventure, the Seraphic Doctor, and learn at the school of the divine Teacher: let us listen to his word of life and truth that resonates in the depths of our soul. Let us purify our thoughts and actions so that he may dwell within us and that we may understand his divine voice which draws us toward true happiness.

## His Teaching[3]

I would like to study some other aspects of the doctrine of St. Bonaventure of Bagnoregio. He is an eminent theologian who deserves to be set beside another great thinker, a contemporary of his, St. Thomas Aquinas. Both scrutinized the mysteries of Revelation, making the most of the resources of human reason, in the fruitful dialogue between faith and reason that characterized the Christian Middle Ages, making it a time of great intellectual vigor, as well as of faith and ecclesial renewal, which is often

---

[3] Pope Benedict XVI, General Audience, March 17, 2010.

not sufficiently emphasized. Other similarities link them: Both Bonaventure, a Franciscan, and Thomas, a Dominican, belonged to the Mendicant Orders which, with their spiritual freshness, as I mentioned in previous Catecheses, renewed the whole Church in the thirteenth century and attracted many followers. They both served the Church with diligence, passion, and love, to the point that they were invited to take part in the Ecumenical Council of Lyons in 1274, the very same year in which they died; Thomas while he was on his way to Lyons, Bonaventure while the Council was taking place.

Even the statues of the two saints in St. Peter's Square are parallel. They stand right at the beginning of the colonnade, starting from the façade of the Vatican Basilica; one is on the left wing and the other on the right. Despite all these aspects, in these two great saints we can discern two different approaches to philosophical and theological research which show the originality and depth of the thinking of each. I would like to point out some of their differences.

A first difference concerns the concept of theology. Both doctors wondered whether theology was a practical or a theoretical and speculative science. St. Thomas reflects on two possible contrasting answers. The first says: theology is a reflection on faith, and the purpose of faith is that the human being become good and live in accordance with God's will. Hence the aim of theology would be to guide people on the right, good road; thus it is basically a practical science. The other position says: theology seeks to know God. We are the work of God; God is above our action. God works right action in us; so it essentially concerns not our own doing but knowing God, not our own actions. St. Thomas's conclusion is: theology entails both aspects: it is theoretical, it seeks to know God ever better, and it is practical, it seeks to orient our life to the good. But there is a primacy of knowledge: above all we must know God and then continue to act in accordance with God (*Summa Theologiae,* 1a, q. 1, art. 4). This primacy of knowledge in comparison with practice is significant to St. Thomas's fundamental orientation.

St. Bonaventure's answer is very similar, but the stress he gives is different. St. Bonaventure knows the same arguments for both directions, as does St. Thomas, but in answer to the question as to whether theology was a practical or a theoretical science, St. Bonaventure makes a triple distinction; he therefore extends the alternative between the theoretical (the primacy of knowledge) and the practical (the primacy of practice), adding a third attitude which he calls "sapiential" and affirming that wisdom embraces both aspects. And he continues: wisdom seeks contemplation (as the highest form of knowledge), and has as its intention "*ut boni fiamus*" that we become good, especially this: to become good (cf. *Breviloquium, Prologus,* 5). He then adds: "faith is in the intellect, in such a way that it provokes affection. For example: the knowledge that Christ died 'for us' does not remain knowledge but necessarily becomes affection, love" (*Proemium in I Sent.,* q. 3).

His defense of theology is along the same lines, namely, of the rational and methodical reflection on faith. St. Bonaventure lists several arguments against engaging in theology perhaps also widespread among a section of the Franciscan friars and also present in our time: that reason would empty faith,

*Thus in the end, for St. Bonaventure, the primacy of love is crucial.*

that it would be an aggressive attitude to the word of God, that we should listen and not analyze the word of God (cf. *Letter of St. Francis of Assisi to St. Anthony of Padua*). The saint responds to these arguments against theology that demonstrate the perils that exist in theology itself saying: it is true that there is an arrogant manner of engaging in theology, a pride of reason that sets itself above the word of God. Yet real theology, the rational work of the true and good theology has another origin, not the pride of reason. One who loves wants to know his beloved better and better; true theology does not involve reason and its research prompted by pride, *"sed propter amorem eius cui assentit* [but is] motivated by love of the One who gave his consent" (*Proemium in I Sent.,* q. 2) and wants to be better acquainted with the beloved: this is the fundamental intention of theology. Thus in the end, for St. Bonaventure, the primacy of love is crucial.

Consequently St. Thomas and St. Bonaventure define the human being's final goal, his complete happiness in different ways. For St. Thomas the supreme end to which our desire is directed is: to see God. In this simple act of seeing God all problems are solved: we are happy, nothing else is necessary.

Instead, for St. Bonaventure the ultimate destiny of the human being is to love God, to encounter him, and to be united in his and our love. For him this is the most satisfactory definition of our happiness.

Along these lines we could also say that the loftiest category for St. Thomas is the true, whereas for St. Bonaventure it is the good. It would be mistaken to see a contradiction in these two answers. For both of them the true is also the good, and the good is also the true; to see God is to love and to love is to see. Hence it was a question of their different interpretation of a fundamentally shared vision. Both emphases have given shape to different traditions and different spiritualities and have thus shown the fruitfulness of the faith: one, in the diversity of its expressions.

Let us return to St. Bonaventure. It is obvious that the specific emphasis he gave to his theology, of which I have given only one example, is explained on the basis of the Franciscan charism. The "Poverello" of Assisi, notwithstanding the intellectual debates of his time, had shown with his whole life the primacy of love. He was a living icon of Christ in love with Christ, and thus he made the figure of the Lord present in his time — he did not convince his contemporaries with his words but rather with his life. In all St. Bonaventure's works, precisely also his scientific works, his scholarly works, one sees and finds this Franciscan inspiration; in other words one notices that his thought starts with his encounter with the "Poverello" of Assisi. However, in order to understand the practical elaboration of the topic "primacy of love" we must bear in mind yet another source: the writings of the so-called Pseudo-Dionysius, a Syrian theologian of the sixth century who concealed himself behind the pseudonym of Dionysius the Areopagite. In the choice of this name he was referring to a figure in the Acts of the Apostles (cf. 17: 34). This theologian had created a liturgical theology and a mystical theology, and had spoken extensively of the different orders of angels. His writings were translated into Latin in the ninth century. At the time of St. Bonaventure we are in the thirteenth century; a new tradition appeared that aroused the interest of the saint and of other theologians of his century. Two things in particular attracted St. Bonaventure's attention.

1. Pseudo-Dionysius speaks of nine orders of angels whose names he had found in Scripture and then organized in his own way, from the simple angels to the seraphim. St. Bonaventure interprets these orders of angels as steps on the human creature's way to God. Thus they can represent the human journey, the ascent toward communion with God. For St. Bonaventure there is no doubt: St. Francis of Assisi belonged to the Seraphic Order, to the supreme Order, to the choir of seraphim, namely, he was a pure flame of love. And this is what Franciscans should have been. But St. Bonaventure knew well that this final step in the approach to God could not be inserted into a juridical order but

is always a special gift of God. For this reason the structure of the Franciscan Order is more modest, more realistic, but nevertheless must help its members to come ever closer to a seraphic existence of pure love. Previously I spoke of this synthesis between sober realism and evangelical radicalism in the thought and action of St. Bonaventure.

2. St. Bonaventure, however, found in the writings of Pseudo-Dionysius another element, an even more important one. Whereas for St. Augustine the *intellectus*, the seeing with reason and the heart, is the ultimate category of knowledge, Pseudo-Dionysius takes a further step: in the ascent toward God one can reach a point in which reason no longer sees. But in the night of the intellect love still sees it sees what is inaccessible to reason. Love goes beyond reason, it sees further, it enters more profoundly into God's mystery. St. Bonaventure was fascinated by this vision which converged with his own Franciscan spirituality. It is precisely in the dark night of the Cross that divine love appears in its full grandeur; where reason no longer sees, love sees. The final words of his "The Journey of the Mind into God," can seem to be a superficial interpretation, an exaggerated expression of devotion devoid of content; instead, read in the light of St. Bonaventure's theology of the Cross, they are a clear and realistic expression of Franciscan spirituality: "If you seek in what manner these things occur (that is, the ascent toward God) interrogate grace, not doctrine, desire, not understanding; the groan of praying, not the study of reading ... not light, but the fire totally inflaming, transferring one into God" (VII 6). All this is neither anti-intellectual nor antirational: it implies the process of reason but transcends it in the love of the Crucified Christ. With this transformation of the mysticism of Pseudo-Dionysius, St. Bonaventure is placed at the source of a great mystical cur-

rent which has greatly raised and purified the human mind: it is a lofty peak in the history of the human spirit.

This theology of the Cross, born of the encounter of Pseudo-Dionysius's theology and Franciscan spirituality, must not make us forget that St. Bonaventure also shares with St. Francis of Assisi his love for creation, his joy at the beauty of God's creation. On this point I cite a sentence from the first chapter of the "Journey": "He who is not brightened by such splendors of created things is blind; he who does not awake at such clamors is deaf; he who does not praise God on account of all these effects is mute; he who does not turn toward the First Principle on account of such indications is stupid" (I, 15).

The whole creation speaks loudly of God, of the good and beautiful God; of his love. Hence for St. Bonaventure the whole of our life is a "journey," a pilgrimage, an ascent to God. But with our own strength alone we are incapable of climbing to the loftiness of God. God himself must help us, must "pull" us up. Thus prayer is necessary. Prayer, says the saint, is the mother and the origin of the upward movement — "*sursum action*," an action that lifts us up, Bonaventure says. Accordingly I conclude with the prayer with which he begins his "Journey": "Let us therefore say to the Lord Our God: 'Lead me forth, Lord, in thy way, and let me step in thy truth; let my heart be glad, that it fears thy name'" (I, 1).

# CHAPTER FIFTEEN

# St. Albert the Great[1]

One of the great masters of medieval theology is St. Albert the Great. The title "Great" (*Magnus*) with which he has passed into history indicates the vastness and depth of his teaching, which he combined with holiness of life. However, his contemporaries did not hesitate to attribute to him titles of excellence even then. One of his disciples, Ulric of Strasbourg, called him the "wonder and miracle of our epoch."

He was born in Germany at the beginning of the thirteenth century. When he was still young he went to Italy, to Padua, the seat of one of the most famous medieval universities. He devoted himself to the study of the so-called "liberal arts": grammar, rhetoric, dialectics, arithmetic, geometry, astronomy and music, that is, to culture in general, demonstrating that characteristic interest in the natural sciences which was soon to become the favorite field for his specialization. During his stay in Padua he attended the Church of the Dominicans, whom he then joined with the profession of the religious vows. Hagiographic sources suggest that Albert came to this decision gradually. His intense relationship with God, the Dominican Friars' example of holiness, hearing the sermons of Bl. Jordan of Saxony, St. Dominic's successor as the Master General of the Order of Preachers, were the decisive factors that helped him to overcome every doubt

---

[1] Pope Benedict XVI, General Audience, March 24, 2010.

and even to surmount his family's resistance. God often speaks to us in the years of our youth and points out to us the project of our life. As it was for Albert, so also for all of us, personal prayer, nourished by the Lord's word, frequent reception of the Sacraments, and the spiritual guidance of enlightened people are the means to discover and follow God's voice. He received the religious habit from Bl. Jordan of Saxony.

After his ordination to the priesthood, his superiors sent him to teach at various theological study centers annexed to the convents of the Dominican Fathers. His brilliant intellectual qualities enabled him to perfect his theological studies at the most famous university in that period, the University of Paris. From that time on St. Albert began his extraordinary activity as a writer that he was to pursue throughout his life.

Prestigious tasks were assigned to him. In 1248 he was charged with opening a theological studium at Cologne, one of the most important regional capitals of Germany, where he lived at different times and which became his adopted city. He brought with him from Paris an exceptional student, Thomas Aquinas. The sole merit of having been St. Thomas's teacher would suffice to elicit profound admiration for St. Albert. A relationship of mutual esteem and friendship developed between these two great theologians, human attitudes that were very helpful in the development of this branch of knowlege. In 1254, Albert was elected Provincial of the Dominican Fathers' "Provincia Teutoniae," Teutonic Province, which included communities scattered over a vast territory in Central and Northern Europe. He distinguished himself for the zeal with which he exercised this ministry, visiting the communities and constantly recalling his confreres to fidelity, to the teaching and example of St. Dominic.

His gifts did not escape the attention of the Pope of that time, Alexander IV, who wanted Albert with him for a certain time at Anagni where the Popes went frequently in Rome itself and at Viterbo, in order to avail himself of Albert's theological advice. The same Supreme Pontiff appointed Albert Bishop of Regensburg, a large and celebrated diocese, but which was going through a difficult period. From 1260 to 1262, Albert exercised this ministry with unflagging dedication, succeeding in restoring peace and harmony to the city, in reorganizing parishes and convents and in giving a new impetus to charitable activities.

In the year 1263–1264, Albert preached in Germany and in Bohemia, at the request of Pope Urban IV. He later returned to Cologne and took up his role as lecturer, scholar, and writer. As a man of prayer, science, and charity, his authoritative intervention in various events of the Church and of the society of the time were acclaimed: above all, he was a man of reconciliation and peace in Cologne, where the Archbishop had run seriously foul of the city's institutions; he did his utmost during the Second Council of Lyons, in 1274, summoned by Pope Gregory X, to encourage union between the Latin and Greek Churches after the separation of the great schism with the East in 1054. He also explained the thought of Thomas Aquinas which had been the subject of objections and even quite unjustified condemnations.

He died in his cell at the convent of the Holy Cross, Cologne, in 1280, and was very soon venerated by his confreres. The Church proposed him for the worship of the faithful with his beatification in 1622 and with his canonization in 1931, when Pope Pius XI proclaimed him Doctor of the Church. This was certainly an appropriate recognition of this great man of God and outstanding scholar, not only of the truths of the faith but of a great many other branches of knowledge; indeed, with a glance at the titles of his very numerous works, we realize that there was something miraculous about his culture and that his encyclopedic interests led him not only to concern himself with philosophy and theology, like other contemporaries of his, but also with every other discipline then known, from physics to chemistry, from astronomy to minerology, from botany to zoology. For this reason Pope Pius XII named him patron of enthusiasts of the natural sciences and also called him "Doctor universalis" precisely because of the vastness of his interests and knowledge.

Of course, the scientific methods that St. Albert the Great used were not those that came to be established in the following centuries. His method consisted simply in the observation, description, and classification of the phenomena he had studied, but it was in this way that he opened the door for future research.

He still has a lot to teach us. Above all, St. Albert shows that there is no opposition between faith and science, despite certain episodes of misunderstanding that have been recorded in history. A man of faith and prayer, as was St. Albert the Great, can serenely foster the study of the natural sciences and progress in knowledge of the micro- and macrocosm, discovering the laws proper to the subject, since all this contributes to fostering thirst for and love of God. The Bible speaks to us of creation as of the first language through which God, who is supreme intelligence, who is the Logos, reveals to us something of himself. The Book of Wisdom, for example, says that the phenomena of nature, endowed with greatness and beauty, are like the works of an artist through which, by analogy, we may know the Author of creation (cf. Wis 13: 5).

With a classical similitude in the Middle Ages and in the Renaissance one can compare the natural world to a book written by God that we read according to the different approaches of the sciences (cf. *Address to the participants in the Plenary Meeting of the Pontifical Academy of Sciences*, October 31, 2008; *L'Osservatore Romano English edition*, November 5, 2008, p. 6). How many scientists, in fact, in the wake of St. Albert the Great, have carried on their research inspired by wonder at and gratitude for a world which, to their eyes as scholars and believers, appeared and appears as the good work of a wise and loving Creator! Scientific study is then transformed into a hymn of praise. Enrico Medi, a great astrophysicist of our time, whose cause of beatification has been introduced, wrote: "O you mysterious galaxies ... I see you, I calculate you, I understand you, I study you and I discover you, I penetrate you and I gather you. From you I take light and make it knowledge, I take movement and make it wisdom, I take sparkling colors and make them poetry; I take you stars in my hands and, trembling in the oneness of my being, I raise you above yourselves and offer you in prayer to the Creator, that through me alone you stars can worship" (*Le Opere. Inno alla creazione*).

St. Albert the Great reminds us that there is friendship between science and faith and that through their vocation to the study of nature, scientists can take an authentic and fascinating path of holiness.

His extraordinary openmindedness is also revealed in a cultural feat which he carried out successfully, that is, the acceptance and appreciation of Aristotle's thought. In St. Albert's time, in fact, knowledge was spreading of numerous works by this great Greek philosopher, who lived a quarter of a century before Christ, especially in the sphere of ethics and metaphysics. They showed the power of reason, explained lucidly and clearly the meaning and structure of reality, its intelligibility, and the value and purpose of human actions. St. Albert the Great opened the door to the complete acceptance in medieval philosophy and theology of Aristotle's philosophy, which was subsequently given a definitive form by St. Thomas. This reception of a pagan pre-Christian philosophy, let us say, was an authentic cultural revolution in that epoch. Yet many Christian thinkers feared Aristotle's philosophy, a non-Christian philosophy, especially because, presented by his Arab commentators, it had been interpreted in such a way, at least in certain points, as to appear completely irreconcilable with the Christian faith. Hence a dilemma arose: are faith and reason in conflict with each other or not?

This is one of the great merits of St. Albert: with scientific rigor he studied Aristotle's works, convinced that all that is truly rational is compatible with the faith revealed in the Sacred Scriptures. In other words, St. Albert the Great thus contributed to the formation of an autonomous philosophy, distinct from theology and united with it only by the unity of the truth. So it was that in the thirteenth century a clear distinction came into being between these two branches of knowledge, philosophy and theology, which, in conversing with each other, cooperate harmoniously in the discovery of the authentic vocation of man, thirsting for truth and happiness: and it is above all theology that St. Albert defined as "emotional knowledge," which points out to human beings their vocation to eternal joy, a joy that flows from full adherence to the truth.

St. Albert the Great was capable of communicating these concepts in a simple and understandable way. An authentic son of St. Dominic, he willingly preached to the People of God, who were won over by his words and by the example of his life.

Dear brothers and sisters, let us pray the Lord that learned theologians will never be lacking in holy Church, wise and devout like St. Albert the Great, and that he may help each one of us to make our own the "formula of holiness" that he followed in his life: "to desire all that I desire for the glory of God, as God desires for his glory all that he desires," in other words always to be conformed to God's will, in order to desire and to do everything only and always for his glory.

# CHAPTER SIXTEEN

# St. Thomas Aquinas

## HIS LIFE [1]

Our main theme for this book is meditation on some of the great thinkers of the Middle Ages. In previous chapters we looked at the great figure of St. Bonaventure, a Franciscan, and now I wish to address the one whom the Church calls the *Doctor communis* — namely, St. Thomas Aquinas. In his Encyclical *Fides et Ratio* my venerable predecessor, Pope John Paul II, recalled that "the Church has been justified in consistently proposing St. Thomas as a master of thought and a model of the right way to do theology" (n. 43). It is not surprising that, after St. Augustine, among the ecclesiastical writers mentioned in the *Catechism of the Catholic Church* St. Thomas is cited more than any other, at least sixty-one times! He was also called the *Doctor Angelicus,* perhaps because of his virtues and, in particular, the sublimity of his thought and the purity of his life.

Thomas was born between 1224 and 1225 in the castle that his wealthy noble family owned at Roccasecca near Aquino, not far from the famous Abbey of Montecassino where his parents sent him to receive the first elements of his education. A few years later he moved to Naples, the capital of the Kingdom of Sicily, where Frederick II had founded a prestigious university. Here the thinking of the Greek philosopher Aristotle was taught

---

[1] Pope Benedict XVI, General Audience, June 2, 2010.

without the limitations imposed elsewhere. The young Thomas was introduced to it and immediately perceived its great value. However, it was above all in those years that he spent in Naples that his Dominican vocation was born. Thomas was in fact attracted by the ideal of the Order recently founded by St. Dominic. However, when he was clothed in the Dominican habit, his family opposed this decision and he was obliged to leave the convent and spend some time at home.

In 1245, by which time he had come of age, he was able to continue on the path of his response to God's call. He was sent to Paris to study theology under the guidance of another saint, Albert the Great, of whom I spoke not long ago. A true and deep friendship developed between Albert and Thomas. They learned to esteem and love each other to the point that Albert even wanted his disciple to follow him to Cologne, where he had been sent by the Superiors of the Order to found a theological *studium*. Thomas then once again came into contact with all Aristotle's works and his Arab commentators that Albert described and explained.

In this period the culture of the Latin world was profoundly stimulated by the encounter with Aristotle's works that had long remained unknown. They were writings on the nature of knowledge, on the natural sciences, on metaphysics, on the soul, and on ethics and were full of information and intuitions that appeared valid and convincing. All this formed an overall vision of the world that had been developed without and before Christ, and with pure reason, and seemed to impose itself on reason as "the" vision itself; accordingly seeing and knowing this philosophy had an incredible fascination for the young. Many accepted enthusiastically, indeed with a critical enthusiasm, this enormous baggage of ancient knowledge that seemed to be able to renew culture advantageously and to open totally new horizons. Others,

however, feared that Aristotle's pagan thought might be in opposition to the Christian faith and refused to study it. Two cultures
converged: the pre-Christian culture of Aristotle with its radical rationality and the classical Christian culture. Certain circles,
moreover, were led to reject Aristotle by the presentation of this
philosopher which had been made by the Arab commentators
Avicenna and Averroës. Indeed, it was they who had transmitted
the Aristotelian philosophy to the Latin world. For example, these
commentators had taught that human beings have no personal
intelligence but that there is a single universal intelligence, a spiritual substance common to all that works in all as "one," hence, a
depersonalization of man. Another disputable point passed on by
the Arab commentators was that the world was eternal like God.
This understandably unleashed never-ending disputes in the university and clerical worlds. Aristotelian philosophy was continu-
ing to spread even among the populace.

Thomas Aquinas, at the school of Albert the Great, did
something of fundamental importance for the history of philosophy and theology, I would say for the history of culture: he
made a thorough study of Aristotle and his interpreters, obtain-
ing for himself new Latin translations of the original Greek texts.
Consequently he no longer relied solely on the Arab commentators but was able to read the original texts for himself. He commented on most of the Aristotelian opus, distinguishing between
what was valid and was dubious or to be completely rejected,
showing its consonance with the events of the Christian Revelation and drawing abundantly and perceptively from Aristotle's
thought in the explanation of the theological texts he was uniting. In short, Thomas Aquinas showed that a natural harmony
exists between Christian faith and reason. And this was the great
achievement of Thomas who, at that time of clashes between two
cultures, that time when it seemed that faith would have to give

in to reason, showed that they go hand in hand, that insofar as reason appeared incompatible with faith it was not reason, and so what appeared to be faith was not faith, since it was in opposition to true rationality; thus he created a new synthesis which formed the culture of the centuries to come.

Because of his excellent intellectual gifts Thomas was summoned to Paris to be professor of theology on the Dominican chair. Here he began his literary production which continued until his death and has something miraculous about it: he commented on Sacred Scripture because the professor of theology was above all an interpreter of Scripture; and he commented on the writings of Aristotle, powerful systematic works, among which stands out his *Summa Theologiae,* treatises and discourses on various subjects. He was assisted in the composition of his writings by several secretaries, including his confrere, Reginald of Piperno, who followed him faithfully and to whom he was bound by a sincere brotherly friendship marked by great confidence and trust. This is a characteristic of saints: they cultivate friendship because it is one of the noblest manifestations of the human heart and has something divine about it, just as Thomas himself explained in some of the *Quaestiones* of his *Summa Theologiae.* He writes in it: "it is evident that charity is the friendship of man for God" and for "all belonging to him" (Vol. II, q. 23, a. 1).

He did not stay long or permanently in Paris. In 1259 he took part in the General Chapter of the Dominicans in Valenciennes where he was a member of a commission that established the Order's program of studies. Then from 1261 to 1265, Thomas was in Orvieto. Pope Urban IV, who held him in high esteem, commissioned him to compose liturgical texts for the Feast of

> *Because of his excellent intellectual gifts Thomas was summoned to Paris to be professor of theology on the Dominican chair.*

*Corpus Christi,* which we are celebrating tomorrow, established subsequent to the Eucharistic miracle of Bolsena. Thomas had an exquisitely Eucharistic soul. The most beautiful hymns that the Liturgy of the Church sings to celebrate the mystery of the Real Presence of the Body and Blood of the Lord in the Eucharist are attributed to his faith and his theological wisdom. From 1265 until 1268 Thomas lived in Rome where he probably directed a *Studium,* that is, a study house of his Order, and where he began writing his *Summa Theologiae* (cf. Jean-Pierre Torrell, *Tommaso d'Aquino. L'uomo e il teologo,* Casale Monf., 1994, pp. 118–184).

In 1269 Thomas was recalled to Paris for a second cycle of lectures. His students understandably were enthusiastic about his lessons. One of his former pupils declared that a vast multitude of students took Thomas's courses, so many that the halls could barely accommodate them; and this student added, making a personal comment, that "listening to him brought him deep happiness." Thomas's interpretation of Aristotle was not accepted by all, but even his adversaries in the academic field, such as Godfrey of Fontaines, for example, admitted that the teaching of Friar Thomas was superior to others for its usefulness and value and served to correct that of all the other masters. Perhaps also in order to distance him from the lively discussions that were going on, his superiors sent him once again to Naples to be available to King Charles I who was planning to reorganize university studies.

In addition to study and teaching, Thomas also dedicated himself to preaching to the people. And the people too came willingly to hear him. I would say that it is truly a great grace when theologians are able to speak to the faithful with simplicity and fervor. The ministry of preaching, moreover, helps theology

scholars themselves to have a healthy pastoral realism and enriches their research with lively incentives.

The last months of Thomas's earthly life remain surrounded
by a particular, I would say, mysterious atmosphere. In December 1273, he summoned his friend and secretary Reginald to
inform him of his decision to discontinue all work because he
had realized, during the celebration of Mass subsequent to a supernatural revelation, that everything he had written until then
"was worthless." This is a mysterious episode that helps us to understand not only Thomas's personal humility, but also the fact
that, however lofty and pure it may be, all we manage to think
and say about the faith is infinitely exceeded by God's greatness
and beauty which will be fully revealed to us in Heaven. A few
months later, more and more absorbed in thoughtful meditation, Thomas died while on his way to Lyons to take part in the
Ecumenical Council convoked by Pope Gregory X. He died in
the Cistercian Abbey of Fossanova, after receiving the Viaticum
with deeply devout sentiments.

The life and teaching of St. Thomas Aquinas could be
summed up in an episode passed down by his ancient biographers. While, as was his wont, the saint was praying before
the Crucifix in the early morning in the chapel of St. Nicholas
in Naples, Domenico da Caserta, the church sacristan, over-
heard a conversation. Thomas was anxiously asking whether
what he had written on the mysteries of the Christian faith
was correct. And the Crucified One answered him: "You have
spoken well of me, Thomas. What is your reward to be?"
And the answer Thomas gave him was what we too, friends
and disciples of Jesus, always want to tell him: "Nothing but
Yourself, Lord!" (*ibid.*, p. 320).

## His Method [2]

St. Thomas Aquinas was a theologian of such value that the study of his thought was explicitly recommended by the Second Vatican Council in two documents, the Decree *Optatam totius* on the Training of Priests, and the Declaration *Gravissimum Educationis,* which addresses Christian Education. Indeed, already in 1880 Pope Leo XIII, who held St. Thomas in high esteem as a guide and encouraged Thomistic studies, chose to declare him Patron of Catholic Schools and Universities.

The main reason for this appreciation is not only explained by the content of his teaching but also by the method he used, especially his new synthesis and distinction between philosophy and theology. The Fathers of the Church were confronted by different philosophies of a Platonic type in which a complete vision of the world and of life was presented, including the subject of God and of religion. In comparison with these philosophies they themselves had worked out a complete vision of reality, starting with faith and using elements of Platonism to respond to the essential questions of men and women. They called this vision, based on biblical revelation and formulated with a correct Platonism in the light of faith, "our philosophy." The word "philosophy" was not, therefore, an expression of a purely rational system and, as such, distinct from faith but rather indicated a comprehensive vision of reality, constructed in the light of faith but used and conceived of by reason; a vision that naturally exceeded the capacities proper to reason but as such also fulfilled it.

For St. Thomas the encounter with the pre-Christian philosophy of Aristotle (who died in about 322 b.c.) opened up a new perspective. Aristotelian philosophy was obviously a philosophy worked out without the knowledge of the Old and

---

[2] Pope Benedict XVI, General Audience, June 16, 2010.

New Testaments, an explanation of the world without revelation through reason alone. And this consequent rationality was convincing. Thus the old form of the Fathers' "our philosophy" no longer worked. The relationship between philosophy and theology, between faith and reason, needed to be rethought. A "philosophy" existed that was complete and convincing in itself, a rationality that preceded the faith, followed by "theology," a form of thinking with the faith and in the faith. The pressing question was this: are the world of rationality, philosophy conceived of without Christ, and the world of faith compatible? Or are they mutually exclusive? Elements that affirmed the incompatibility of these two worlds were not lacking, but St. Thomas was firmly convinced of their compatibility indeed that philosophy worked out without the knowledge of Christ was awaiting, as it were, the light of Jesus to be complete. This was the great "surprise" of St. Thomas that determined the path he took as a thinker. Showing this independence of philosophy and theology and, at the same time, their reciprocal relationality was the historic mission of the great teacher. And thus it can be understood that in the nineteenth century, when the incompatibility of modern reason and faith was strongly declared, Pope Leo XIII pointed to St. Thomas as a guide in the dialogue between them. In his theological work, St. Thomas supposes and concretizes this relationality. Faith consolidates, integrates, and illumines the heritage of truth that human reason acquires. The trust with which St. Thomas endows these two instruments of knowledge, faith and reason, may be traced back to the conviction that both stem from the one source of all truth, the divine *Logos,* which is active in both contexts, that of Creation and that of redemption.

Together with the agreement between reason and faith, we must recognize on the other hand that they avail themselves of different cognitive procedures. Reason receives a truth by virtue of its intrinsic evidence, mediated or unmediated; faith, on the contrary, accepts a truth on the basis of the authority of the Word of God that is revealed. St. Thomas writes at the beginning of his *Summa Theologiae:* "We must bear in mind that there are two kinds of sciences. There are some which proceed from a principle known by the natural light of the intelligence, such as arithmetic and geometry and the like. There are some which proceed from principles known by the light of a higher science: thus the science of perspective proceeds from principles established by geometry, and music from principles established by arithmetic. So it is that sacred doctrine is a science, because it proceeds from principles established by the light of a higher science, namely, the science of God and the blessed" (ia, q. 1, a. 2).

This distinction guarantees the autonomy of both the human and the theological sciences. However, it is not equivalent to separation but, rather, implies a reciprocal and advantageous collaboration. Faith, in fact, protects reason from any temptation to distrust its own abilities, stimulates it to be open to ever broader horizons, keeps alive in it the search for foundations and, when reason itself is applied to the supernatural sphere of the relationship between God and man, faith enriches his work. According to St. Thomas, for example, human reason can certainly reach the affirmation of the existence of one God, but only faith, which receives the divine Revelation, is able to draw from the mystery of the Love of the Triune God.

Moreover, it is not only faith that helps reason. Reason too, with its own means can do something important for faith, making it a threefold service which St. Thomas sums up in the preface to his commentary on the *De Trinitate* of Boethius: "demonstrating those truths that are preambles of the faith; giving a clearer notion, by certain similitudes, of the truths of the faith; resisting those who speak against the faith, either by showing that their statements are false, or by showing that they are not necessarily true" (q. 2, a. 3). The entire history of theology is basically the exercise of this task of the mind which shows the intelligibility of faith, its articulation and inner harmony, its reasonableness and its ability to further human good. The correctness of theological reasoning and its real cognitive meaning is based on the value of theological language which, in St. Thomas's opinion, is principally an analogical language. The distance between God, the Creator, and the being of his creatures is infinite; dissimilitude is ever greater than similitude (cf. DS 806). Nevertheless in the whole difference between Creator and creatures an analogy exists between the created being and the being of the Creator, which enables us to speak about God with human words.

St. Thomas not only based the doctrine of analogy on exquisitely philosophical argumentation but also on the fact that with the Revelation God himself spoke to us and therefore authorized us to speak of him. I consider it important to recall this doctrine. In fact, it helps us get the better of certain objections of contemporary atheism which denies that religious language is provided with an objective meaning and instead maintains that it has solely a subjective or merely emotional value. This objection derives from the fact that positivist thought is convinced that man does not know being but solely the functions of reality that can be experienced. With St. Thomas and with the great philosophical tradition we are convinced that, in reality, man does not only know the functions, the object of the natural sciences, but also knows something of being itself — for example, he knows the person, the You of the other, and not only the physical and biological aspect of his being.

In the light of this teaching of St. Thomas theology says that however limited it may be, religious language is endowed with sense because we touch being like an arrow aimed at the reality it signifies. This fundamental agreement between human reason and Christian faith is recognized in another basic principle of Aquinas's thought. Divine Grace does not annihilate but presupposes and perfects human nature. The latter, in fact, even after sin, is not completely corrupt but wounded and weakened. Grace, lavished upon us by God and communicated through the Mystery of the Incarnate Word, is an absolutely free gift with which nature is healed, strengthened, and assisted in pursuing the innate desire for happiness in the heart of every man and of every woman. All the faculties of the human being are purified, transformed and uplifted by divine Grace.

*In other words, the human, theological, and moral virtues are rooted in human nature.*

An important application of this relationship between nature and Grace is recognized in the moral theology of St. Thomas Aquinas, which proves to be of great timeliness. At the center of his teaching in this field, he places the new law which is the law of the Holy Spirit. With a profoundly evangelical gaze he insists on the fact that this law is the Grace of the Holy Spirit given to all who believe in Christ. The written and oral teaching of the doctrinal and moral truths transmitted by the Church is united to this Grace. St. Thomas, emphasizing the fundamental role in moral life of the action of the Holy Spirit, of Grace, from which flow the theological and moral virtues, makes us understand that all Christians can attain the lofty perspectives of the "Sermon on the Mount," if they live an authentic relationship of faith in Christ, if they are open to the action of his Holy Spirit. However, Aquinas adds, "Although Grace is more efficacious than nature, yet nature is more essential to man, and therefore more enduring" (*Summa Theologiae, Ia–IIae*, q. 94, a. 6, ad 2), which is why, in the Christian moral perspective, there is a place for reason which is capable of discerning natural moral law. Reason can recognize this by considering what it is good to do and what it is good to avoid in order to achieve that felicity which everyone has at heart, which also implies a responsibility toward others and, therefore, the search for the common good. In other words, the human, theological, and moral virtues are rooted in human nature. Divine Grace accompanies, sustains, and impels ethical commitment but, according to St. Thomas, all human beings, believers and nonbelievers alike, are called to recognize the needs of human nature expressed in natural law and to draw inspiration from it in the formulation of positive laws, namely those issued by the civil and political authorities to regulate human coexistence.

When natural law and the responsibility it entails are denied, this dramatically paves the way to ethical relativism at the individual level and to totalitarianism of the State at the political level. The defence of universal human rights and the affirmation of the absolute value of the person's dignity postulate a foundation. Does not natural law constitute this foundation, with the non-negotiable values that it indicates? Ven. John Paul II wrote in his Encyclical *Evangelium Vitae* words that are still very up to date: "It is therefore urgently necessary, for the future of society and the development of a sound democracy, to rediscover those essential and innate human and moral values which flow from the very truth of the human being and express and safeguard the dignity of the person: values which no individual, no majority and no State can ever create, modify or destroy, but must only acknowledge, respect and promote" (n. 71).

To conclude, Thomas presents to us a broad and confident concept of human reason: *broad* because it is not limited to the spaces of the so-called "empirical-scientific" reason, but open to the whole being and thus also to the fundamental and inalienable questions of human life; and *confident* because human reason, especially if it accepts the inspirations of Christian faith, is a promoter of a civilization that recognizes the dignity of the person, the intangibility of his rights and the cogency of his or her duties. It is not surprising that the doctrine on the dignity of the person, fundamental for the recognition of the inviolability of human rights, developed in schools of thought that accepted the legacy of St. Thomas Aquinas, who had a very lofty conception of the human creature. He defined it, with his rigorously philosophical language, as "what is most perfect to be found in all nature — that is, a subsistent individual of a rational nature" (*Summa Theologiae,* 1a, q. 29, a. 3).

The depth of St. Thomas Aquinas's thought let us never forget it flows from his living faith and fervent piety, which he expressed in inspired prayers such as this one in which he asks God: "Grant me, O Lord my God, a mind to know you, a heart to seek you, wisdom to find you, conduct pleasing to you, faithful perseverance in waiting for you, and a hope of finally embracing you."

### HIS TEACHING [3]

Even more than 700 years after St. Thomas Aquinas's death we can learn much from him. My predecessor, Pope Paul VI, also said this, in a discourse he gave at Fossanova on September 14, 1974, on the occasion of the seventh centenary of St. Thomas's death. He asked himself: "Thomas, our Teacher, what lesson can you give us?" And he answered with these words: "trust in the truth of Catholic religious thought, as defended, expounded and offered by him to the capacities of the human mind" (*L'Osservatore Romano English Edition* [ore], September 26, 1974, p. 4). In Aquino moreover, on that same day, again with

---

[3] Pope Benedict XVI, General Audience, June 23, 2010.

reference to St. Thomas, Paul VI said, "all of us who are faithful sons and daughters of the Church can and must be his disciples, at least to some extent!" (*Address to people in the Square at Aquino*, September 14, 1974; *ORE*, p. 5).

Let us too, therefore, learn from the teaching of St. Thomas and from his masterpiece, the *Summa Theologiae*. It was left unfinished, yet it is a monumental work: it contains 512 questions and 2,669 articles. It consists of concentrated reasoning in which the human mind is applied to the mysteries of faith, with clarity and depth, to the mysteries of faith, alternating questions with answers in which St. Thomas deepens the teaching that comes from Sacred Scripture and from the Fathers of the Church, especially St. Augustine. In this reflection, in meeting the true questions of his time, which are also often our own questions, St. Thomas, also by employing the method and thought of the ancient philosophers, and of Aristotle in particular, thus arrives at precise, lucid, and pertinent formulations of the truths of faith in which truth is a gift of faith, shines out, and becomes accessible to us for our reflection. However, this effort of the human mind — Aquinas reminds us with his own life — is always illumined by prayer, by the light that comes from on high. Only those who live with God and with his mysteries can also understand what they say to us.

In the *Summa* of theology, St. Thomas starts from the fact that God has three different ways of being and existing: God exists in himself, he is the beginning and end of all things, which is why all creatures proceed from him and depend on him: then God is present through his Grace in the life and activity of the Christian, of the saints; lastly, God is present in an altogether special way in the Person of Christ, here truly united to the man Jesus, and active in the Sacraments that derive from his work of redemption. Therefore, the structure of this monumental work (cf. Jean-Pierre Torrell, *La "Summa" di San Tommaso,* Milan 2003, pp. 29–75), a quest with "a theological vision" for the fullness of God (cf. *Summa Theologiae,* Ia q. 1, a. 7), is divided into three parts and is illustrated by the *Doctor Communis* himself St. Thomas with these words: "Because the chief aim of sacred doctrine is to teach the knowledge of God, not only as he is in himself, but also as he is the beginning of things and their last end, and especially of rational creatures, as is clear from what has already been said, therefore, we shall treat: (1) Of God; (2) Of the rational creature's advance toward God; (3) Of Christ, Who as man, is our way to God" (*ibid.,* I, q. 2). It is a circle: God in himself, who comes out of himself and takes us by the hand, in such a way that with Christ we return to God, we are united to God, and God will be all things to all people.

The First Part of the *Summa Theologiae* thus investigates God in himself, the mystery of the Trinity and of the creative activity of God. In this part we also find a profound reflection on the authentic reality of the human being, inasmuch as he has emerged from the creative hands of God as the fruit of his love. On the one hand we are dependent created beings, we do not come from ourselves; yet, on the other, we have a true autonomy so that we are not only something apparent as certain Platonic philosophers say but a reality desired by God as such and possessing an inherent value.

In the Second Part St. Thomas considers man, impelled by Grace, in his aspiration to know and love God in order to be happy in time and in eternity. First of all the Author presents the theological principles of moral action, studying how, in the free choice of the human being to do good acts, reason, will, and passions are integrated, to which is added the power given by God's Grace through the virtues and the gifts of the Holy Spirit, as well as the help offered by moral law. Hence the human being is a dynamic being who seeks himself, seeks to become himself, and, in this regard, seeks to do actions that build him up, that make him truly man; and here the moral law comes into it. Grace and reason itself, the will, and the passions enter too. On this basis St. Thomas describes the profile of the man who lives in accordance with the Spirit and thus becomes an image of God.

Here Aquinas pauses to study the three theological virtues faith, hope, and charity, followed by a critical examination of more than fifty moral virtues, organized around the four cardinal virtues prudence, justice, temperance, and fortitude. He then ends with a reflection on the different vocations in the Church.

In the Third Part of the *Summa,* St. Thomas studies the Mystery of Christ the way and the truth through which we can reach God the Father. In this section he writes almost unparalleled pages on the Mystery of Jesus's Incarnation and Passion, adding a broad treatise on the seven sacraments, for it is in them that the Divine Word Incarnate extends the benefits of the Incarnation for our salvation, for our journey of faith toward God and eternal life. He is, as it were, materially present with the realities of creation, and thus touches us in our inmost depths.

In speaking of the sacraments, St. Thomas reflects in a special way on the Mystery of the Eucharist, for which he had such great devotion, the early biographers claim, that he would lean his head against the Tabernacle, as if to feel the throbbing of Jesus's divine and human heart. In one of his works, commenting on Scripture, St. Thomas helps us to understand the excellence of the sacrament of the Eucharist, when he writes: "Since this [the Eucharist] is the sacrament of Our Lord's Passion, it contains in itself the Jesus Christ who suffered for us. Thus, whatever is an effect of Our Lord's Passion is also an effect of this sacrament. For this sacrament is nothing other than the application of Our Lord's Passion to us" (cf. *Commentary on John,* chapter 6, lecture 6, n. 963). We clearly understand why St.

Thomas and other saints celebrated Holy Mass shedding tears of compassion for the Lord who gave himself as a sacrifice for us, tears of joy and gratitude.

Dear brothers and sisters, at the school of the saints, let us fall in love with this sacrament! Let us participate in Holy Mass with recollection, to obtain its spiritual fruits, let us nourish ourselves with this Body and Blood of Our Lord, to be ceaselessly fed by divine Grace! Let us willingly and frequently linger in the company of the Blessed Sacrament in heart-to-heart conversation!

All that St. Thomas described with scientific rigor in his major theological works, such as, precisely, the *Summa Theologiae,* and the *Summa contra gentiles,* was also explained in his preaching, both to his students and to the faithful. In 1273, a year before he died, he preached throughout Lent in the Church of San Domenico Maggiore in Naples. The content of those sermons was gathered and preserved: they are the *Opuscoli* in which he explains the *Apostles' Creed,* interprets the Prayer of the *Our Father,* explains the *Ten Commandments,* and comments on the *Hail Mary.*

The content of the Doctor Angelicus's preaching corresponds with virtually the whole structure of the *Catechism of the Catholic Church.* Actually, in catechesis and preaching, in a time like ours of renewed commitment to evangelization, these fundamental subjects should never be lacking: what *we believe,* and here is the Creed of the faith; what *we pray,* and here is the *Our Father* and the *Hail Mary;* and what *we live,* as we are taught by biblical Revelation, and here is the law of the love of God and neighbor and the *Ten Commandments,* as an explanation of this mandate of love.

I would like to propose some simple, essential, and convincing examples of the content of St. Thomas's teaching. In his booklet on *The Apostles' Creed* he explains the value of faith. Through it, he says, the soul is united to God and produces, as it were, a shot of eternal life; life receives a reliable orientation, and we overcome temptations with ease. To those who object that faith is foolishness because it leads to belief in something that does not come within the experience of the senses, St. Thomas gives a very articulate answer and recalls that this is an inconsistent doubt, for human intelligence is limited and cannot know everything. Only if we were able to know all visible and invisible things perfectly would it be genuinely foolish to accept truths out of pure faith. Moreover, it is impossible to live, St. Thomas observes, without trusting in the experience of others, wherever one's own knowledge falls short. It is thus reasonable to believe in God, who reveals himself, and to the testimony of the Apostles: they were few, simple, and poor, grief-stricken by the Crucifixion of their Teacher. Yet many wise, noble, and rich people converted very soon after hearing their preaching. In fact this is a miraculous phenomenon of history, to which it is far from easy to give a convincing answer other than that of the Apostles' encounter with the Risen Lord.

In commenting on the article of the Creed on the Incarnation of the divine Word, St. Thomas makes a few reflections. He says that the Christian faith is strengthened in considering the mystery of the Incarnation; hope is strengthened at the thought that the Son of God came among us, as one of us, to communicate his own divinity to human beings; charity is revived because there is no more obvious sign of God's love for us than the sight of the Creator of the universe making himself a creature, one of us. Finally, in contemplating the mystery of God's Incarnation,

*Only if we were able to know all visible and invisible things perfectly would it be genuinely foolish to accept truths out of pure faith.*

we feel kindled within us our desire to reach Christ in glory. Using a simple and effective comparison, St. Thomas remarks: "If the brother of a king were to be far away, he would certainly long to live beside him. Well, Christ is a brother to us; we must therefore long for his company and become of one heart with him" (*Opuscoli teologico-spirituali*, Rome 1976, p. 64).

In presenting the prayer of the *Our Father*, St. Thomas shows that it is perfect in itself, since it has all five of the characteristics that a well-made prayer must possess: trusting, calm abandonment; a fitting content because, St. Thomas observes, "it is quite difficult to know exactly what it is appropriate and inappropriate to ask for, since choosing among our wishes puts us in difficulty" (*ibid.*, p. 120); and then an appropriate order of requests, the fervor of love, and the sincerity of humility.

Like all the saints, St. Thomas had a great devotion to Our Lady. He described her with a wonderful title: *Triclinium totius Trinitatis; triclinium,* that is, a place where the Trinity finds rest since, because of the Incarnation, in no creature as in her do the three divine Persons dwell and feel delight and joy at dwelling in her soul full of Grace. Through her intercession we may obtain every help.

With a prayer that is traditionally attributed to St. Thomas and that in any case reflects the elements of his profound Marian devotion we too say: "O most Blessed and sweet Virgin Mary, Mother of God ... I entrust to your merciful heart ... my entire life.... Obtain for me as well, O most sweet Lady, true charity with which from the depths of my heart I may love your most Holy Son, our Lord Jesus Christ, and, after him, love you above all other things ... and my neighbor, in God and for God."

# CHAPTER SEVENTEEN

# John Duns Scotus[1]

I would like to present another important figure in the history of theology. He is Bl. John Duns Scotus, who lived at the end of the thirteenth century. An ancient epitaph on his tombstone sums up the geographical coordinates of his biography: "Scotland bore me, England received me, France taught me, Cologne in Germany holds me." We cannot disregard this information, partly because we know very little about the life of Duns Scotus. He was probably born in 1266 in a village called, precisely, "Duns," near Edinburgh.

Attracted by the charism of St. Francis of Assisi, he entered the Family of the Friars Minor and was ordained a priest in 1291. He was endowed with a brilliant mind and a tendency for speculation which earned him the traditional title of *Doctor subtilis,* "Subtle Doctor." Duns Scotus was oriented to the study of philosophy and theology at the famous Universities of Oxford and of Paris. Having successfully completed his training, he embarked on teaching theology at the Universities of Oxford and Cambridge and then of Paris, beginning by commenting, like all the bachelors of theology of his time, on the *Sentences* of Peter Lombard. Indeed, Duns Scotus's main works are the mature fruit of these lessons and take the name of the places where he taught: *Ordinatio* (called in the past *Opus Oxoniense* — Oxford), *Reportatio*

---

[1] Pope Benedict XVI, General Audience, July 7, 2010.

*Cantabrigiensis* (Cambridge), *Reportata Parisiensia* (Paris). One can add to these at least the *Quodlibeta* (or *Quaestiones quodlibetales*), a quite important work consisting of twenty-one questions on various theological subjects. Duns Scotus distanced himself from Paris, after a serious dispute broke out between King Philip IV the Fair and Pope Boniface VIII, rather than sign a document hostile to the Supreme Pontiff as the King requested of all religious, preferring voluntary exile. Thus he left the country, together with the Franciscan Friars, out of love for the See of Peter.

This event invites us to remember how often in the history of the Church believers have met with hostility and even suffered persecution for their fidelity and devotion to Christ, to the Church, and to the Pope. We all look with admiration at these Christians who teach us to treasure as a precious good faith in Christ and communion with the Successor of Peter, hence with the universal Church.

However, friendly relations between the King of France and the successor of Boniface VIII were soon restored and in 1305 Duns Scotus was able to return to Paris to lecture on theology with the title of *Magister regens* [regent master], now we would say "Professor." Later his superiors sent him to Cologne as Professor of the Franciscan *Studium* of Theology, but he died on November 8, 1308, when he was only forty-three years old, leaving nevertheless a consistent opus.

Because of the fame of his holiness, his cult soon became widespread in the Franciscan Order, and Ven. Pope John Paul II, wishing to confirm it, solemnly beatified him on March 20, 1993, describing him as the "minstrel of the Incarnate Word and defender of Mary's Immaculate Conception" (*Solemn Vespers,* St. Peter's Basilica; *L'Osservatore Romano English Edition* [ore], n. 3, 24 March 1993, p. 1). These words sum up the important contribution that Duns Scotus made to the history of theology.

First of all he meditated on the Mystery of the Incarnation and, unlike many Christian thinkers of the time, held that the Son of God would have been made man even if humanity had not sinned. He says in his *Reportatio Parisiensis*: "To think that God would have given up such a task had Adam not sinned would be quite unreasonable! I say, therefore, that the fall was not the cause of Christ's predestination and that if no one had fallen, neither the angel nor man in this hypothesis Christ would still have been predestined in the same way" (in *III Sent.*, d. 7, 4). This perhaps somewhat surprising thought crystallized because, in the opinion of Duns Scotus, the Incarnation of the Son of God, planned from all eternity by God the Father at the level of love is the fulfilment of creation and enables every creature, in Christ and through Christ, to be filled with grace and to praise and glorify God in eternity. Although Duns Scotus was aware that in fact, because of original sin, Christ redeemed us with his Passion, Death, and Resurrection, he reaffirmed that the Incarnation is the greatest and most beautiful work of the entire history of salvation, that it is not conditioned by any contingent fact but is God's original idea of ultimately uniting with himself the whole of creation, in the Person and Flesh of the Son.

As a faithful disciple of St. Francis, Duns Scotus liked to contemplate and preach the Mystery of the saving Passion of Christ, as the expression of the loving will, of the immense love of God who reaches out with the greatest generosity, irradiating his goodness and love (cf. *Tractatus de primo principio,* c. 4). Moreover this love was not only revealed on Calvary but also in the Most Blessed Eucharist, for which Duns Scotus had a very deep devotion and which he saw as the Sacrament of the Real Presence of Jesus and as the Sacrament of unity and communion that induces us to love each other and to love God, as the Supreme Good we have in common (cf. *Reportatio Parisiensis,* in *IV Sent.,* d. 8, q. 1, n. 3). As I wrote in my Letter for the International Congress in Cologne marking the seventh centenary of the death of Bl. Duns Scotus, citing the thought of our author: "just as this love, this charity, was at the origin of all things, so too our eternal happiness will be in love and charity alone: 'willing, or the loving will, is simply eternal life, blessed and perfect'" (*AAS* 101 [2009], 5).

Dear brothers and sisters, this strongly "Christocentric" theological vision opens us to contemplation, wonder and gratitude: Christ is the center of history and of the cosmos; it is he who gives meaning, dignity, and value to our lives! As Pope Paul VI proclaimed in Manila, I too would like to cry out to the world: [Christ] "reveals the invisible God, he is the firstborn of all creation, the foundation of everything created. He is the Teacher of mankind, and its Redeemer. He was born, he died and he rose again for us. He is the center of history and of the world; he is the one who knows us and who loves us; he is the companion and the friend of our life.... I could never finish speaking about him" (*Homily,* Mass at Quezon Circle, Manila; November 29, 1970).

Not only Christ's role in the history of salvation but also that of Mary is the subject of the *Doctor subtilis's* thought. In the times of Duns Scotus the majority of theologians countered with an objection that seemed insurmountable, the doctrine which holds that Mary Most Holy was exempt from original sin from the very first moment of her conception: in fact, at first sight the universality of the Redemption brought about by Christ might seem to be jeopardized by such a statement, as though Mary had had no need of Christ or his redemption. Therefore the theologians opposed this thesis. Thus, to enable people to understand this preservation from original sin, Duns Scotus developed an argument that was later, in 1854, also to be used by Bl. Pope

Pius IX when he solemnly defined the Dogma of the Immaculate Conception of Mary. And this argument is that of "preventive Redemption," according to which the Immaculate Conception is the masterpiece of the Redemption brought about by Christ because the very power of his love and his mediation obtained that the Mother be preserved from original sin. Therefore Mary is totally redeemed by Christ, but already before her conception. Duns Scotus's confreres, the Franciscans, accepted and spread this doctrine enthusiastically, and other theologians, often with a solemn oath, strove to defend and perfect it.

In this regard I would like to highlight a fact that I consider relevant. Concerning the teaching on the Immaculate Conception, important theologians like Duns Scotus enriched what the People of God already spontaneously believed about the Blessed Virgin and expressed in acts of devotion, in the arts, and in Christian life in general with the specific contribution of their thought. Thus faith both in the Immaculate Conception and in the bodily Assumption of the Virgin was already present in the People of God, while theology had not yet found the key to interpreting it in the totality of the doctrine of the faith. The People of God therefore precede theologians, and this is all thanks *May theologians always be ready to listen to this source of faith and retain the humility and simplicity of children!* to that supernatural *sensus fidei*, namely, that capacity infused by the Holy Spirit that qualifies us to embrace the reality of the faith with humility of heart and mind. In this sense, the People of God is the "teacher that goes first" and must then be more deeply examined and intellectually accepted by theology. May theologians always be ready to listen to this source of faith and retain the humility and simplicity of children! I mentioned this before, saying: "There have been great scholars, great experts, great theologians, teachers of faith who have taught us many things. They have gone into the details of Sacred Scripture ... but have been unable to see the mystery itself, its central nucleus.... The essential has remained hidden!... On the other hand, in our time there have also been 'little ones' who have understood this mystery. Let us think of St. Bernadette Soubirous; of St. Thérèse of Lisieux, with her new interpretation of the Bible that is 'non-scientific' but goes to the heart of Sacred Scripture" (*Homily, Mass for the Members of the International Theological Commission*, Pauline Chapel, Vatican City, December 1, 2009).

Lastly, Duns Scotus has developed a point to which modernity is very sensitive. It is the topic of freedom and its relationship with the will and with the intellect. Our author underlines freedom as a fundamental quality of the will, introducing an approach that lays greater emphasis on the will. Unfortunately, in later authors, this line of thinking turned into a voluntarism, in contrast to the so-called "Augustinian and Thomist intellectualism." For St. Thomas Aquinas, who follows St. Augustine, freedom cannot be considered an innate quality of the will, but, the fruit of the collaboration of the will and the mind. Indeed, an idea of innate and absolute freedom — as it evolved, precisely, after Duns Scotus — placed in the will that precedes the intellect, both in God and in man, risks leading to the idea of a God who would not even be bound to truth and good. The wish to save God's absolute transcendence and diversity with such a radical and impenetrable accentuation of his will does not take into account that the God who revealed himself in Christ is the God "Logos," who acted and acts full of love for us.

Of course, as Duns Scotus affirms, love transcends knowledge and is capable of perceiving ever better than thought, but it is always the love of the God who is "Logos" (cf. Benedict XVI, *Address at the University of Regensburg*, September 12, 2006). In the human being too, the idea of absolute freedom, placed in the will, forgetting the connection with the truth, does not know that freedom itself must be liberated from the limits imposed on it by sin. All the same, the Scotist vision does not fall into these extremes: for Duns Scotus a free act is the result of the concourse of intellect and will, and if he speaks of a "primacy" of the will, he argues this precisely because the will always follows the intellect.

In speaking to Roman seminarians, I recalled that "Since the beginning and throughout all time but especially in the modern age freedom has been the great dream of humanity" (*Discourse at the Roman Major Seminary,* February 20, 2009). Indeed, in addition to our own daily experience, modern history actually teaches us that freedom is authentic and helps with building a truly human civilization only when it is reconciled with truth. If freedom is detached from truth, it becomes, tragically, a principle of the destruction of the human person's inner harmony, a source of prevarication of the strongest and the violent and a cause of suffering and sorrow. Freedom, like all the faculties with which the human being is endowed, increases and is perfected, Duns Scotus says, when the human being is open to God, making the most of the disposition to listen to his voice: when we listen to divine Revelation, to the word of God in order to accept it, a message reaches us that fills our life with light and hope and we are truly free.

Dear brothers and sisters, Bl. Duns Scotus teaches us that in our life the essential is to believe that God is close to us and loves us in Jesus Christ, and therefore to cultivate a deep love for him and for his Church. We on earth are witnesses of this love. May Mary Most Holy help us to receive this infinite love of God which we will enjoy eternally to the full in Heaven, when our soul is at last united to God for ever in the Communion of Saints.

# Books by Pope Benedict XVI
## from Our Sunday Visitor

### The Apostles
Hardback and Paperback

### The Fathers, Volume I
St. Clement to St. Augustine

### The Fathers, Volume II
St. Leo to St. Bernard

### The Apostles, Illustrated

### The Fathers, Illustrated
Volume I – St. Clement to St. Paulinus of Nola
Volume II – St. Augustine to St. Maximus the Confessor

### Breakfast with Benedict

### Questions and Answers

### Saint Paul the Apostle

### The Virtues

Our Sunday Visitor Publishing
1-800-348-2440 ◆ www.osv.com